# WARSAW, LODZ, VILNA
## The Holocaust Ghettos

**Linda Jacobs Altman**

**Enslow Publishers, Inc.**
40 Industrial Road
Box 398
Berkeley Heights, NJ 07922
USA

http://www.enslow.com

Originally published as *The Holocaust Ghettos* in 1998.

**Library of Congress Cataloging-in-Publication Data**

Altman, Linda Jacobs, 1943– author.
    Warsaw, Lodz, Vilna : the Holocaust ghettos / Linda Jacobs Altman.
        p. cm. — (Remembering the Holocaust)
    Includes bibliographical references and index.
    ISBN 978-0-7660-6207-8
    1. Holocaust, Jewish (1939–1945)—Juvenile literature. 2. World War,
1939–1945—Concentration camps—Juvenile literature. 3. Jews—
Persecutions—Germany—History—20th century—Juvenile literature. 4. Jews—
Persecutions—Poland—History—20th century—Juvenile literature. I. Title.
    D804.3.A454 2014
    940.53'18538—dc23
                         2014007405

**Future Editions:**
Paperback ISBN: 978-0-7660-6208-5
EPUB ISBN: 978-0-7660-6209-2
Single-User PDF ISBN: 978-0-7660-6210-8
Multi-User PDF ISBN: 978-0-7660-6211-5

Printed in the United States of America
072014 HF Group, North Manchester, IN
10 9 8 7 6 5 4 3 2 1

**To Our Readers:** We have done our best to make sure all Internet addresses in this
book were active and appropriate when we went to press. However, the author and the
publisher have no control over and assume no liability for the material available on
those Internet sites or on other Web sites they may link to. Comments can be sent by
e-mail to comments@enslow.com or to the address on the back cover.

**Illustration Credits:** Created by Enslow Publishers, Inc., p. 7; National Archives and
Records Administration (NARA), p. 1; National Archives Collection of WWII War
Crime Records, Entry 1, United States Counsel for the Prosecution of Axis Criminality,
United States Evidence Files, 1945–46, PS-1061 (Stroop Report), pp. 4, 81.

**Cover Illustration:** National Archives and Records Administration (NARA):
SS soldiers guarding a column of captive Jews in the Warsaw ghetto. The liquidation
of the Warsaw ghetto after an uprising. The photo is taken from Jürgen Stroop's
report to Heinrich Himmler in May of 1943. The German original title reads:
"forcibly pushed out of the shelter."

# CONTENTS

*Many Jewish resistance fighters were killed by SS guards during the Warsaw uprising. Here, a group of resistance fighters surrenders to a Nazi patrol.*

# Introduction

# THE ALL-CONSUMING FIRE

When World War II ended in 1945, a nameless horror became apparent: the deliberate murder of approximately 6 million European Jews and 5 million Gypsies, Poles, Slavs, and others by the forces of Nazi Germany. This war-within-a-war came to be known as the Holocaust, from the word meaning "wholesale destruction and loss of life, especially by fire."[1]

The period of Nazi domination began on January 30, 1933, when a rabble-rouser named Adolf Hitler became chancellor of Germany, second in command to President Paul von Hindenburg. Hitler was a vicious anti-Semite who believed that the Nordic peoples, or "Aryans" as he called them, were a master race, destined to rule the world. The Jews were destined only to die, and the rest of the world's "inferior" peoples to serve as slave labor for the Aryan masters.

He promised the German people a glorious Third Reich (government or "empire"): the Holy Roman Empire was the first Reich; the unified German Empire of Prince Otto von Bismarck, the second. Now would come Nazi Germany, with Adolf Hitler as its *führer*, its absolute leader. This grandiose plan ended on the battlefields of World War II, and in the gas chambers of the concentration camps.

Hitler did not invent anti-Semitism, nor did he force it on an unwilling public. For centuries, European Jews were persecuted by the Christian majority. In 1096, Crusaders on their way to kill Muslim nonbelievers in Palestine slaughtered thousands of Rhineland Jews as "Christ killers." The charge was more than a thousand years old, based upon the belief that Jewish leaders had plotted the death of Jesus. When a deadly epidemic of bubonic plague swept through Europe in the fourteenth century, the terrified populace killed Jews, claiming they had poisoned the wells.

Martin Luther, leader of the Protestant Reformation in the sixteenth century, decried the very existence of the Jews. He hated them because they refused to accept Jesus as the messiah (savior) of all humankind:

> What shall we Christians do now with this depraved and damned people of the Jews? . . . I will give my faithful advice: First, that one should set fire to their synagogues. . . . Then that one should also break down and destroy their houses. . . . That one should drive them out of the country.[2]

Adolf Hitler harnessed this hatred and placed it at the center of his Nazi ideology. Jewishness, said the führer, was not simply a religious or cultural identity; it was "in the blood," a matter of race. A Jew could not cease being Jewish by converting to Christianity and assimilating or blending

**German Administration of Eastern Europe 1942**

☐ = Countries occupied by Germany in 1942
☐ = Unoccupied countries in 1942

SWEDEN

Baltic Sea

Riga

REICHSKOMMISSARIAT OSTLAND

Kovno

Vilna

SOVIET UNION

PART OF SOVIET UNION UNDER GERMAN MILITARY ADMINISTRATION

DANZIG WEST PRUSSIA

EAST PRUSSIA

Minsk

BIALYSTOK
Bialystok

GREATER GERMANY

WARTHEGAU
Lodz

Warsaw

Theresienstadt

UPPER SILESIA

GENERAL GOVERNMENT

Lvov

REICHSKOMMISSARIAT UKRAINE

PROTECTORATE OF BOHEMIA AND MORAVIA

SLOVAKIA

HUNGARY

ROMANIA

Sea of Azov

ITALY

CROATIA

SERBIA

Black Sea

into German culture. Hitler made no secret of his intentions toward members of this "poisonous" race; they must be eliminated if Germany was to achieve "greatness."

Once he became chancellor, Hitler wasted no time in seeking this goal. On April 1, 1933, he mounted a symbolic one-day boycott of Jewish businesses all over Germany, and in May, he presided at a mass rally against Jewish intellectuals. Amid the pomp and splendor of martial music and torchlight parades, screaming Nazis burned books by Jewish authors and others who opposed the regime.

President von Hindenburg died on August 2, 1934. A new law that had been passed just a day earlier combined the offices of chancellor and president. Under that law, Hitler took power. He promptly did away with the title of president, to become known as führer, absolute dictator of the German nation. When that happened, the fate of the Jewish people and the German nation was sealed.

On September 15, 1935, the Nuremberg Laws were approved by the Nazi-controlled national assembly. These laws deprived Jews of German citizenship and excluded them from most areas of the German economy. Many fled the country at that time, some to safety in America and others to surrounding countries. There they would once again face destruction when the Nazi forces overran Europe.

The Jews have always been a resilient people, able to affirm life in the face of persecution and death. When things were bad, Jews thanked God that they weren't worse. When things got worse, they comforted one another with the thought that "this too shall pass." For countless generations, that ability to adjust and to endure has been one of their strengths.

The Nazis used this strength against them. To keep the Jews from open revolt, the Nazis hid their true intentions as long as possible. The ghettos (areas of cities where Jews were forced to live) played an important role in that strategy. In these grim areas, Jews could be isolated and controlled while the Nazis set the stage for genocide (the systematic killing of an entire racial, ethnic, political, or religious group).

The ghettos would exist for less than four years. The order that created them was issued on September 21, 1939; the order that liquidated them was issued on July 21, 1943. During that period, at various times, small ghettos were created and quickly eliminated, their populations either killed outright or sent to one of the larger ghettos. The United

States Holocaust Memorial Museum recognizes nine major ghettos:[3]

1. Bialystok (Poland)
2. Kovno (Lithuania)
3. Lodz (Poland)
4. Lvov (Poland)
5. Minsk (Belorussia)
6. Riga (Latvia)
7. Theresienstadt (Czechoslovakia)
8. Vilna (Lithuania)
9. Warsaw (Poland)

In these hellish places, simply going about the ordinary business of life was an act of courage and defiance. Thousands starved to death or died of disease; some killed themselves; and some were shot down in the streets. Some fought back, although they knew the battle was hopeless.

Ultimately, the story of the ghettos, like that of the Holocaust itself, stands as a memorial to the victims and a warning to the rest of us that such things must never again be allowed to happen.

# SEPTEMBER 1939: THE HORROR BEGINS

A dolf Hitler knew how to keep his enemies guessing. He was a master of saying one thing, doing another, and somehow escaping the consequences. Germany took over Austria and Czechoslovakia in 1938. The world watched and did nothing. On September 1, 1939, German troops launched a massive invasion of Poland, triggering all-out war in Europe.

Troops and tanks attacked from the ground; planes attacked from the air. The German army quickly pounded Poland into submission. Just three weeks after the invasion, on September 21, 1939, a fateful order came down from Nazi headquarters: The Jews of Poland should be "concentrated" in designated areas, and a *Judenrat* (Jewish Council) appointed to implement Nazi orders within each Jewish community.

## Reinhard Heydrich and the Ghettos

The ghetto order came from Reinhard Heydrich, a former naval intelligence officer with a psychopathic personality and an almost total lack of human feeling. Heydrich was expelled from the navy in 1931 for misconduct. Less than a year later, he had become an important member of the SS (*Schutzstaffel*), Hitler's personal guard unit. Members of the SS were also known as the "black shirts," because of their uniforms. Heydrich formed a security division of the SS, called the SD (*Sicherheitsdienst*).

The original function of the SD was to oversee the loyalty and behavior of the Nazi party membership. Heydrich built the SD into a vast surveillance network, using hidden microphones and thousands of informers to keep watch. Under his leadership, children informed on their parents, friends betrayed friends, workers watched suspicious-looking coworkers.

Together with the Gestapo (short for *Geheime Staatspolizei*, "Secret State Police"), the SD spread terror all over Germany and Europe. Heydrich used the same cold-blooded efficiency with which he built the SD to establish the ghettos. The first ghetto was created in Poland in the autumn of 1939; the last was created in Budapest on November 13, 1944. Heydrich knew from the beginning that the ghettos would be a short-term solution to a long-term problem. Jews would be gathered from the countryside and isolated from the Gentile population. The ultimate fate of these Jews remained to be decided, but Heydrich ordered that ghettos be located near railway lines to make liquidation easier.

The order set forth the bare outlines of how a ghetto should be organized and governed. The specifics depended upon local conditions. Some ghettos were walled; some encircled by barbed wire. Some had invisible walls in the form of posted boundaries that were not to be crossed except under specified conditions. Some ghettos allowed Gentiles to enter in the course of their normal business; others did not.

The first step in isolating the Jews from the rest of the population was to identify and mark them for easy recognition. Many Orthodox Jews were Hasidim and readily spotted by their black garb, their full beards, and their Yiddish language. Yiddish is a blend of Hebrew and German, written in Hebrew characters. But not all Jews could be so easily identified. Despite Hitler's insistence that the Jews were a race, there were thousands who simply did not "look Jewish."

To deal with this embarrassing "problem," the Nazis required all Jews to wear a special badge on their outer garments. In Warsaw, it was a white ribbon imprinted with a blue Star of David. In Kovno, it was "a yellow Shield of David, diameter 8–10 centimeters [about 3 inches]."[1] Any Jew caught without the badge was subject to immediate arrest.

Once symbolically separated from the rest of society, the Jews were systematically impoverished. The Nazis confiscated their homes, businesses, and life savings. With nowhere to go and no way to support themselves, the Jews put up little resistance when they were "resettled" into ghettos.

Wearing badges or armbands and living in segregated neighborhoods was nothing new to the Jews of Europe. In the thirteenth century, the Church required them to wear a yellow star. In the 1400s, many nations of Christian Europe forced Jews into ghettos. In the eighteenth century, Catherine the Great of Russia restricted Jews to a specific area which became known as the Pale of Settlement.

The purpose of this discriminatory treatment was to protect Christians from nonbelievers, and to prevent Jews from gaining too much economic or political power. There was prejudice, brutality, and even murder in this suppression but there was not systematic extermination.

Looking to their own history, the Jews had reason to believe that this latest oppression would be much like all those which had gone before. Be patient, they told one another. Endure. This too shall pass.

They were wrong.

## Piotrkow: The First Ghetto

German forces entered the Polish city of Piotrkow, near Lodz, on September 5, 1939. They stormed the predominantly Jewish section of the city, setting fires and shooting Jews who ran out of the burning buildings. When the fires had turned to embers, squads of soldiers entered homes that had escaped the flames to rob and kill the occupants.

These soldiers had been exposed to anti-Semitic propaganda for years. They were not only ready to kill, but to be pitiless and vicious in all their dealings with Jews. To them, killing was like a sport. One group ordered six captured Jews to run, then shot them as they fled. On the eve of Rosh Hashanah (the Jewish New Year), which fell on September 13 that year, the occupation forces ordered all Jews to be off the streets by 5:00 P.M. At least one man was shot dead because he was five minutes late getting home.

On October 8, 1939, Piotrkow became the site of the first Jewish ghetto of the Nazi era. In what would become a familiar pattern, Jews who lived outside the designated area were forced to move into the ghetto. No sooner was the ghetto established than it began to fill with Jewish refugees from surrounding towns, who were trying to flee the Germans.

While the Judenrat of Piotrkow struggled to provide for the ghetto's ever-growing population, the German military commander of the city presented them with a decree from Hans Frank, governor-general of the region. They were to pay 350,000 zlotys (Polish money) into the treasury within a matter of hours. Three Jews were held hostage to ensure payment.

This huge sum was only the beginning; no sooner had the council delivered the money than the Germans demanded more. In addition to cash payments, they wanted huge quantities of foodstuffs: flour, sugar, butter, eggs. The Jews of Piotrkow ghetto went hungry in order to meet the demands of the anti-Semites who held them captive.

## Establishing the Lodz Ghetto

Before the war, 233,000 Jews lived in Lodz, a third of the city's total population. It was the second-largest Jewish community in Poland. As soon as the Nazis occupied the city, the military government established a Jewish Council and began planning for a ghetto.

On November 11, 1939, the German occupation authorities called a meeting of the Lodz Jewish Council. The Jews who had been selected to serve assembled at the appointed place. They weren't able to get much work done that day because a Gestapo official sat in on the meeting and at every opportunity berated and insulted the members.

The next morning, twenty council members were ordered to the Gestapo office. They arrived not knowing what to expect and were promptly placed under arrest. Only five survived the horrors of a Gestapo jail.

In February 1940, the Germans set aside two of the most neglected districts in Lodz to serve as a Jewish ghetto. The area contained a total of 31,721 apartments, most of them nothing more than single rooms without running water. More than 160,000 Jews were crammed into this dismal neighborhood. The Nazis took over their homes and any valuables that could not be removed. On May 1, 1940, the ghetto was sealed behind a hastily erected barbed wire fence; any Jew who approached that fence could be shot without warning.

The Germans justified the abominable conditions in the ghetto by claiming that it was a quarantine facility, intended to protect the public from epidemics spread by Jews. Portraying Jews as naturally "infectious" was a favorite tactic of the Nazis.

In November 1940, a propaganda film called *The Eternal Jew* was shown in Germany and the occupied countries. Scene after scene cut back and forth between groups of Jews and hordes of particularly repulsive-looking rats. The message was clear: both Jews and rats were vermin, infecting the world with their filth.

Given the lack of sanitation, medical care, and decent food, the Lodz ghetto was, in fact, a breeding ground for disease. Between May 1, when the ghetto was sealed, and the end of 1940, 6,560 Jews died in Lodz, nearly four times the number that perished in an entire year before the Nazi occupation.

## Warsaw: The Beginning of a Legend

The largest ghetto of the Holocaust was Warsaw. An eight-foot-high wall encircled a sealed quarantine area of about one hundred city blocks. Nearly a half million Jews struggled to survive in the face of incredible odds. There, a small band of survivors mounted a doomed rebellion, choosing to die fighting rather than being shipped like cattle to death camps.

The quarantine area was officially established in October 1940. On October 12, when Jews were observing Yom Kippur (Day of Atonement), the holiest day of the Jewish year, loudspeakers blared the news through the neighborhood: Gentiles had to move out and Jews had to move in. The entire operation was to be accomplished in just a few weeks. It was a time of confusion and fear, of dashing about, and never quite knowing what was going on.

"We move along the earth like men condemned to death," teacher Chaim Kaplan wrote in his diary on October 28, 1939.[2] On November 15, 1940, the ghetto was sealed; Jews couldn't leave without special permits and Gentiles couldn't enter. Kaplan and a few others began to sense the scope of the danger.

> The gigantic catastrophe which has descended on Polish Jewry has no parallel, even in the darkest periods of Jewish history. First, in the depth of the hatred. This is not just hatred . . . which was invented for political purposes. It is a hatred of emotion . . . which imagines the object of hatred to be unclean. . . . The masses have absorbed this sort of qualitative hatred. . . . [They believe that] the Jew is filthy; the Jew is a swindler and an evildoer; . . . the Jew is Satan.[3]

## Emmanuel Ringelblum, Chronicler of the Warsaw Ghetto

Two months after the Nazis conquered Poland in September 1939, historian Emmanuel Ringelblum began to keep a record of the occupation in Warsaw. He was well suited to the task. Part scholar and part social activist, the thirty-nine-year-old Ringelblum had a hunger for truth and a talent for research. He had already published four books and countless articles in scholarly journals.

In the ghetto, Ringelblum formed a circle called the *Oneg Shabbat* ("Joy of Sabbath"). He chose the name carefully, to hide the group's true purpose from the Nazis. The name sounded like that of a religious discussion group. In fact, this group was a well-organized archival committee dedicated to recording and preserving a social history of the ghetto.

Keeping such a record was not an appealing job, but it was one that somebody had to do. Emmanuel Ringelblum was determined to leave a record that would pay tribute to the dead and warn the living about the dangers of racism and hatred. The Oneg Shabbat Archive would be the result of Ringelblum's determination.

# Governing the Ghetto

When the Nazis created ghettos, they needed an efficient way to keep them under control. Rather than tie down German troops to do the job, the Nazis established a Judenrat and an *Ordnungsdienst* ("Order Service"), or Jewish police, in each ghetto.

This Jewish administration answered to a German commander, who answered in turn to the General Government, a Nazi-created administrative area that covered all of central Poland, including the major cities of Krakow and Warsaw.

The role of these Jewish officials has been a subject of great interest to Holocaust historians. They were placed in an impossible situation, between saving their own people and Nazi genocide. In that moral no-man's land, they had to follow even the most brutal orders while rationing dwindling resources in order to keep the people in the ghetto alive.

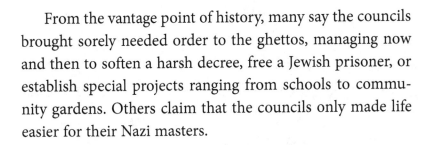

From the vantage point of history, many say the councils brought sorely needed order to the ghettos, managing now and then to soften a harsh decree, free a Jewish prisoner, or establish special projects ranging from schools to community gardens. Others claim that the councils only made life easier for their Nazi masters.

## Forming the Councils

The usual way to form a Judenrat was to select a prominent member of the local Jewish community and order him to compile a list of suitable candidates. This process was not always what it seemed, as the fate of the first council in the Tarnopol ghetto in the Ukraine demonstrates.

The German commandant summoned teacher Mark Gotfried to headquarters and ordered him to select at least sixty prominent Jews to serve on the Tarnopol Council. Sixty-three men followed Gotfried to Nazi headquarters and walked into a nightmare. German soldiers were ready and waiting. Laughing and jeering, they beat the Jews and forced them into trucks. After driving out of town, the soldiers gunned down their unarmed prisoners. Only Gotfried and two elderly men lived to tell about the massacre. Those picked for the second Tarnopol Council were understandably reluctant to serve.

Even without the threat of sudden death, most Jews had no desire to be part of a Nazi-controlled council. The Jews of Ejszyszki in Lithuania selected their council members by lot, like a lottery. In the Russian ghetto Vilna, the rabbi told those selected for the council to accept as if offering themselves for *kiddush hashem* ("sanctification of God's name"), or martyrdom.

In Warsaw, Rabbi Yitzhak Nissenbaum called for *kiddush hahayim* ("the sanctity of life"). By this he meant that the best response to the Nazi threat was not to die for the Jewish faith, but to survive for the Jewish people. Simply staying alive was, in its own way, an act of resistance.

## The Fine Art of Survival

Early in the existence of the ghettos, most Jewish councils were direct and outspoken with the occupation authorities. It took time for them to realize that the Nazis followed neither the law nor ethics in their dealings with Jews.

Zalman Tenenbaum, chairman of the Piotrkow Council, sent a memo to the authorities protesting ghetto conditions: "Starving people, weakened by persistent freezing weather, . . . [living] without the most elementary conditions of hygiene . . . are liable to cause an explosion of epidemics."[1] He received no reply and the ghetto got no relief.

The council in Warsaw had an early and sobering encounter with the Nazi policy of collective responsibility, which held all Jews responsible for the behavior of every individual Jew. Any act of disobedience or defiance brought down punishment on the entire community. For example, when a Jew with a criminal record killed a Polish policeman, the German authorities promptly levied a fine of 300,000 zlotys against the entire Jewish community. To ensure payment, the Germans took fifty-three hostages, who would be shot if the council did not do exactly as ordered.

The council made the payment with a clear statement that it did so under duress: "The Jewish population cannot and will not accept the proposition that all Jews are collectively responsible for the act of an individual Jew. . . . We are

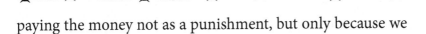

paying the money not as a punishment, but only because we are forced to."[2]

Statements such as this may have soothed Jewish feelings, but they did nothing to alter German behavior. The Nazis did not honor their side of the agreement and executed all fifty-three hostages after the payment was made. The Nazis were masterful manipulators, using people's weaknesses and even their strengths against them. Collective responsibility kept open resistance to a minimum; lies and clever deception made victims cooperate in their own annihilation.

The Nazis were experts at stringing people along: cooperate and you'll be safe; cooperate and things will get better; cooperate and you can live in peace. At first, the Nazis demanded only property, in the form of money and valuables. The Jewish administration gave it to them. Then they demanded slave labor, and the administration gave them that. Finally, they demanded people for deportation, and the councils were in no position to refuse.

The Nazis called deportation "resettlement." The Jews were headed for labor colonies or farming cooperatives, they said. There they would have good food, decent housing, and honorable work until the end of the war. In the beginning, the councils believed these stories. They were easier to accept than the dark rumors of mass executions and extermination camps. "They say . . . that in Slonim [the Nazis] gathered . . . fourteen thousand people—women, children, men—and all were machine-gunned," penned twenty-five-year-old Calel Perechodnik. "Is it possible to believe such a thing? To shoot without reason women, innocent children? Just like that? In full daylight? . . . who would . . . aim their machine guns at helpless, small children? . . . How can the world remain silent? It is probably not true."[3]

The Nazis knew that people would rather believe a lie than face an unthinkable truth. They took that into account when they picked leaders for the Judenrat in each ghetto. They needed men who believed that the Jews had a chance for survival and would pass that belief on to the community. People who clung to hopes for the future would not be eager to risk everything on open revolt.

## To Save at Least a Few

The Nazis chose fifty-nine-year-old Adam Czerniakow to lead the Warsaw Judenrat. By profession, Czerniakow was an engineer: well-educated, clear-minded, sensible to a fault. Because he based his own actions on the logic of a situation, he expected others to do the same. The Nazis probably thought they could use that cautious habit of mind to their own advantage. In some ways, they were right.

Czerniakow's fundamental goal was to outlast the Nazi occupation and save as many Jewish lives as possible through any means necessary. In pursuit of that goal, he did not hesitate to make unpopular decisions such as levying taxes, conscripting workers, and granting or withholding special requests. Many Jews in the ghetto hated him for actions they considered high-handed and insensitive, but Czerniakow was the ultimate realist. He knew a no-win situation when he saw one, and he was not given to fighting impossible battles.

Czerniakow also knew that a thin line separated necessary cooperation from criminal collaboration. Whatever happened, he did not intend to be forced across that line. On the day he took office, he placed twenty-four deadly cyanide capsules in a locked drawer of his desk: one for himself and one for each of the twenty-three councilmen. He fully expected that the day would come when suicide would be the only honorable alternative to helping the Nazis kill thousands of Jews.

In the meantime, Czerniakow conducted himself with quiet dignity in his dealings with the Nazis. With the people of the ghetto, he tried to be compassionate when possible, strict when necessary. One of his earliest and most controversial actions was to supply the Nazis with forced labor. In the early days of the ghetto, German troops filled their labor battalions by grabbing anybody they could find: children, the elderly, the handicapped, sick or injured.

Czerniakow proposed an alternative idea: The Judenrat would supply a daily quota of workers if the Germans stopped kidnapping people off the streets. His idea was to replace chaos with an orderly process that would be less disruptive to the community. To this end, the council appointed organizers and crew chiefs to recruit and supervise the work brigades.

This new agency issued work permits, set the number of hours each person was expected to work, and saw to it that crews were assembled and ready when the Nazis wanted them. Without Czerniakow's intending it, this labor bureaucracy became the nucleus of the much-despised Jewish ghetto police.

Also unintentionally, but with Czerniakow's permission, anyone with money could escape work details by paying a poor Jew to go in his place. Many ghetto inmates became "professional substitutes," selling their labor for the price of a loaf of bread. This was usually the only way a Jew could earn money for work; the Germans paid no wages.

In supplying forced labor, Adam Czerniakow believed he was making ghetto life more endurable. Jews had to work without pay under terrible conditions, but at least they did not have to worry about getting snatched off the street. Substitutes carried more than their share of the load, but at least they earned a pittance to stave off starvation for one more day.

Not everyone in the ghetto agreed with this position. Organizing evil might have made it neater, cleaner, and more efficient, but it did not make it right. Slave labor was slave labor, no matter who set up the work brigades. Many Jews simply refused to show up when they were ordered to report for work. To fill their daily quota, the council sent the Jewish police to track down no-shows or find replacements.

The council also imposed a variety of taxes and fees to pay for ghetto social service programs. This created a gulf between the people and their Jewish leadership. Diarist Chaim Kaplan called the Warsaw Judenrat:

> Strangers in our midst, foreign to our spirit . . . the president of the *Judenrat* and his advisers are muscle-men who were put on our backs by strangers. Most of them are nincompoops whom no one knew in normal times. . . . All their lives until now they were outside the Jewish fold; they did not rejoice in our happiness nor mourn our misfortunes.[4]

## "Rescue Through Work"

Even people who didn't like Adam Czerniakow generally regarded him as an honorable man placed in an untenable position. This was not the case with Mordecai Chaim Rumkowski of Lodz. Appointed "Eldest of the Jews" on

October 13, 1939, he was approaching seventy years old, silver-haired and dignified, with a tendency to dramatize himself and the importance of his role.

Rumkowski transformed the ghetto into his own little dictatorship, keeping tight control of everything from work assignments to food rations. They called him "King Chaim" because of his high-handed style among his fellow Jews. To the Germans, he was deferential. "May a Jew speak?" was his way of addressing them. He portrayed the ghetto as a kind of workers' paradise, a place where hard-working Jews took care of themselves while making a valuable contribution to the German economy. "We have gold currency in the Ghetto!" he once boasted. "The labor of our hands is our gold!" When someone pointed out that this was a German theory, Rumkowski immediately replied: "We're willing to learn from everyone."[5]

The "Eldest of the Jews" of Lodz never missed an opportunity to hold steadfast to his vision for an enduring community of Jewish workers: "Our children and children's children will proudly remember the names of all those who contributed to the creation of the most important Jewish achievement in the ghetto: the labor opportunities which grant justification to live."[6]

Rumkowski wasn't alone in his ideas about the life-saving value of work. Jacob Gens of the Vilna ghetto called upon the people to "increase the output of the workers and thus enhance the justification for our existence."[7] Ephraim Barasz of Bialystok echoed the same theme: "Steps have to be taken so that our 35,000 inhabitants achieve justification [for their existence], so that we may be tolerated."[8]

The rescue-through-work proponents apparently failed to realize that they were playing a deadly game against an opponent who made all the rules. According to those rules, Jewish life *had* no value, and nothing the councils could do would change that.

## The Jewish Police

In the town of Otwock, close in proximity to Warsaw, Calel Perechodnik made a fateful decision: "In February 1941, seeing that the war was not coming to an end and in order to be free from the roundup for labor camps, I entered the ranks of the Ghetto Polizei [ghetto police]."[9]

At the time, joining the force seemed to be a sensible choice. Ghetto police not only escaped the brutal slave labor camps, but got better food rations for themselves and their families. Aiding his family was the deciding factor for Calel Perechodnik. He thought that by joining the police, he could better protect his wife and baby daughter. Like many who took this "opportunity," Perechodnik did not realize how high a price he would pay.

In Warsaw, the Jewish police began operations at the end of November 1940, just two weeks after the ghetto was sealed. At first, the people of the ghetto welcomed them. Chaim Kaplan wrote glowing praise for these "strong, bona fide policemen from among our brothers, to whom you can speak in Yiddish!" Jewish policemen might yell at people, he noted, but "a Jewish shout is not the same as a Gentile one. The latter is coarse, crude, nasty; the former, while it may be threatening, contains a certain gentility, as if to say: 'Don't you understand?'"[10]

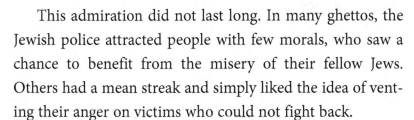

This admiration did not last long. In many ghettos, the Jewish police attracted people with few morals, who saw a chance to benefit from the misery of their fellow Jews. Others had a mean streak and simply liked the idea of venting their anger on victims who could not fight back.

Ghetto police collected taxes and conscripted workers for the forced labor crews. They arrested starving Jews for smuggling food into the ghetto, confiscated property that had been declared contraband, and reported anyone who advocated resistance to German directives. In the Bialystok ghetto, the Jewish police took away bread ration cards as punishment for the "crime" of an untidy yard. In Bedzin, a town near Krakow, the Jewish police arrested the parents of people who failed to report for forced labor, and held them in the ghetto jail.

Ghetto policing was harsh duty that brought out the worst in those who performed it. Emmanuel Ringelblum concluded that the Jewish police of Warsaw were "fearfully corrupt." Corruption extended through every level of the department. "This is because . . . recruits had to pay [the chief of police] to be taken on. The result was that a very bad element was accepted in the police force."[11]

Not all ghetto policemen and council members were self-serving and dishonest. Many were normal everyday people, neither evil nor heroic, trapped between an enemy they despised and a community they could not protect. Under such conditions, even the most decent among them were not always just or fair, and they were never comfortable with the role they were forced to play.

# THE SHAPE OF OUR DAYS

*I was of the opinion that regardless of what was going on in the world, every individual ought to and needs to live normally, work, earn a livelihood, and so forth.*

—*Calel Perechodnik*[1]

This desire to live normally was strong in Jewish tradition. Through centuries of anti-Semitism, Jews had learned to conduct their lives under a dark cloud. Persecution might be just around the corner, but there was still work to be done, children to educate, holidays to observe. There was life to be lived.

In the first days of the ghetto, Jews expected to survive Nazi oppression, using the same stubborn endurance that had served them in the past. They soon realized that the old methods would not work with this relentless new enemy.

Hardship was the basic reality of the ghetto. People crowded together, seven or eight to a one-room apartment without heat or indoor plumbing. Disease and starvation made death rates soar. In the Lodz ghetto, 8,200 Jews died in 1940, the first full year of German occupation. By 1942, there were 13,000 deaths in just the first seven months.[2]

## "Don't Give Up Your Ration Card"

In the grimy streets of the Warsaw ghetto, with death everywhere around, a young beggar sang a song. Over and over, he repeated the words in his clear child's voice: "I'm not giving up my ration . . . card/there . . . are better times a-coming."[3] Passersby nodded in knowing sympathy and threw coins at his feet. "Giving up your ration card" was ghetto slang for dying. With his simple lyric, the threadbare young singer offered a message of hope and defiance.

The Nazis set up the rationing system; the Jewish councils administered it in their respective ghettos. The daily allotment in most ghettos amounted to two or three slices of bread and a bowl of watery soup per person. This food wasn't free; people had to buy their allotments at the going rate.

In some ghettos, they also had to pay a tax on the ration card itself. The Lublin Judenrat charged ten groszy (pennies) for each food card issued. In Warsaw, the tax was one zloty per month, but Adam Czerniakow arranged exemptions for 150,000 of the poorest people in the ghetto. The Jewish councils used this tax money to set up soup kitchens for those who could not afford to buy food anywhere else. Destitute Jews sometimes traded a ten-day ration card for a single meal at one of these soup kitchens.

According to a 1941 survey, poor Jews in the Warsaw ghetto clung to life on as little as 600 to 800 calories per day

for months at a time. Council employees, Jewish police, and workers in "essential" industries received larger allotments.

"Everything revolves around bread and death," claims an old Jewish proverb. That was never more true, or more literal, than in the ghetto. Desperate people held off reporting deaths so they could use the dead person's ration card as long as possible. This tactic was so widespread that it could distort mortality figures, as noted in the Lodz chronicle for July 31, 1942, when cards were issued:

> Today 95 deaths were registered. That figure, so high in relation to the number of deaths that have been occurring in recent days, is eloquent testimony to the populace's making every last possible use of the ration cards belonging to the deceased. It should be realized that today bread was issued for an eight-day period, and that until yesterday one could obtain a ten-day allotment of food. This is a sad but nonetheless telling sign of life in the ghetto.[4]

The problem got worse over time. Old people collapsed in the streets. Children with hollow eyes begged bread from passing strangers. People who had managed to hang on to some of their assets sold or bartered them to buy unrationed food from outside the ghetto. In Kovno, starving Jews went to the wire fence to barter for food with Lithuanians on the "Aryan" side. Jews caught gate-trading, as it was called, could be executed on the spot.

## A Sickness Unto Death

Malnutrition, overcrowding, and lack of public sanitation spawned epidemics of contagious diseases. People endured slow starvation only to die from typhus, tuberculosis, or some other opportunistic infection. There was no cure for these epidemic diseases; ghetto doctors could do little more than ease their patients' passing. Every outbreak worked to the advantage of the Nazis; Jews are carriers of deadly disease, they would say to the Aryans. Don't pity them, don't mingle with them or trade with them; they are shut off in ghettos for your protection.

The Nazis had been laying the groundwork for this approach since Hitler came to power. In 1935, a respected German physician had compared Jews with the organism that causes tuberculosis: "There is a resemblance between Jews and tubercle bacilli: nearly everyone harbors tubercle bacilli, and nearly every people of the earth harbors the Jews; furthermore, an infection can only be cured with difficulty."[5]

Typhus, a deadly disease spread by body lice, swept the Warsaw ghetto in 1941, with 300 cases reported for the month of October alone. In the face of rampant disease, the Nazis launched a massive "public education" program aimed at the Gentile population. In a report to his superiors in Berlin, Warsaw district governor Ludwig Fischer made the thrust of the program clear: "The main purpose of the campaign to explain . . . the dangers of typhus . . . was to point out that the Jews are the disseminators of typhus. The principal slogan of the campaign is 'The Jews - Lice - Typhus.'"[6]

This simplistic propaganda worked because it was, in a very limited sense, true. There was a typhus epidemic among the Jews. The Nazis produced the conditions that led to it, and withheld the sanitation measures to prevent it and the medicines to treat it. Then they loudly announced this "proof" that Jews were dangerous carriers of disease.

## Rules and Regulations

Fascism is a one-party dictatorship in which the state controls every part of life. There is private ownership of property, but the government controls how that property is used. In Germany, the Nazis set up vast bureaucracies, with a department of this, a bureau of that, and a detailed set of rules for everything.

In the ghettos, the Nazis went out of their way to issue absurdly restrictive, even conflicting, directives. Basically, any time Jews walked down the street they were probably in violation of some edict from the authorities. A sampling of directives from the Kovno ghetto shows how petty these endless rules became:

Order No. 1 of the Governor of Kovno, dated July 28, 1941, stated that:

1. The Jewish population is forbidden to walk on the sidewalks. Jews must walk on the right side of the road and go one behind the other.
2. The Jewish population is forbidden to enter promenade walks and public parks. Likewise they are forbidden to use the benches.
3. The Jewish population is forbidden to use public means of transport such as taxicabs, horse carriages, buses, passenger steamers, and similar vehicles. The owners and operators of all public conveyances must display in a visible place a sign reading: "Forbidden to Jews."[7]

Some time later, Jews were forbidden to walk with their hands in their pockets, go to the public market before 10:00 A.M., own furs, or have small electrical appliances in

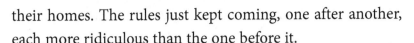

their homes. The rules just kept coming, one after another, each more ridiculous than the one before it.

Regulations systematically isolated and impoverished the Jews, while giving zealous Nazis an excuse for cruelty. For example, many ghettos required male Jews to remove their hats when encountering a German soldier. In Lublin, the authorities posted notices forbidding Jews to salute in just this fashion. Soldiers with nothing better to do used this regulation to torment passing Jews. "Some . . . people who fail to salute . . . are being beaten," explained Emmanuel Ringelblum. "Those who do take their hats off are dragged over to the nearest poster and shown that they were not supposed to."[8]

## To Grow in Knowledge and Wisdom

In the midst of this horror and pain, Jews struggled to hold on to their essential humanity and even their hope for the future. Nowhere was this more apparent than in the many educational projects arranged in the ghettos. Jewish parents believed their children should go to school, no matter how hard life might be.

Just three days after the sealing of the Vilna ghetto, a group of teachers got together to create a school. With the help of their students, they cleaned out rubble, repaired walls, and scavenged for usable materials to create classrooms. By ordinary standards, these classrooms were very crude. Students sat on the floor because they had no chairs and huddled together for warmth against the bitter Polish winter. Still, they studied and learned; the makeshift school system grew.

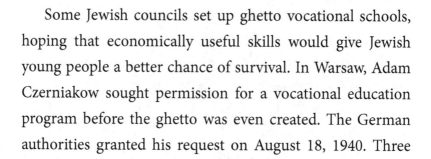
Some Jewish councils set up ghetto vocational schools, hoping that economically useful skills would give Jewish young people a better chance of survival. In Warsaw, Adam Czerniakow sought permission for a vocational education program before the ghetto was even created. The German authorities granted his request on August 18, 1940. Three days later, the first courses opened for enrollment. At the time, Czerniakow truly believed he had found a way to save Jewish lives.

Arranging for academic or religious education was more difficult than setting up vocational schools. The German authorities often gave permission for schools and then later withdrew it with little or no explanation. Not to be outdone, teachers and students found ways to meet in secret.

Teachers conducted primary classes in their homes under the guise of "day care." Just about any institution that served children could be used for educational programs, from refugee homes and orphan asylums to public kitchens. The Nazis apparently failed to notice the large number of unemployed teachers who flocked to such places.

"Jewish children learn in secret," wrote Chaim Kaplan. "We are allowed to feed, direct, and train them; but to educate them is forbidden. . . . In times of danger the children learn to hide their books. Jewish children are clever . . . they hide their books . . . between their trousers and their stomachs, then button their . . . coats. This is a tried-and-true method."[9]

## "One Does Not Present Shows in Cemeteries"

In the harsh world of the ghetto, concerts, plays, and even street entertainments gave people a few precious moments of enjoyment. For a time, they could forget Nazis, ration cards, and forced labor brigades. For a time, they could feel normal again.

In the Kovno ghetto, the Nazi administration refused to allow a full-time orchestra on the grounds that it would take participants away from more important work. Instead, a handful of musicians assigned to the Jewish police started an informal "police orchestra." Soon the group was performing regularly, and every musician who moved to the ghetto was recruited into the force. The Nazis did not seem to notice how many policemen were rehearsing music rather than patrolling the streets.

Every ghetto had its "street singers." Some were panhandlers, hoping to attract a few small coins. Others were first-rate performers down on their luck. In his chronicle of the Lodz ghetto, Lucjan Dobroszycki tells of a street performer named Jankele Herszkowicz who became a star of sorts with his song "Rumkowski, Chaim," which was about the ghetto's leader. He was able to earn a living for several months by performing that song and once even received a gift of money from Rumkowski himself. Another time, the ghetto "troubadour" received a package of matzoh (unleavened bread eaten during Passover) from Rumkowski when he was performing his song in front of a store visited by Rumkowski before the holidays.[10]

The Lodz House of Culture was constantly busy, staging weekly concerts by world-class musicians, such as symphony conductor Theodor Ryder and pianist Leopold Birkenfeld. Chaim Rumkowski issued instructions that all newly arrived musicians, singers, actors, and painters register so their talents could be utilized in the community. The Warsaw ghetto had similar public concerts, along with five professional theater companies that sold out every performance.

In Vilna, the opening of a theater triggered opposition from many residents of the ghetto. Stage plays and other public entertainments seemed out of place in a community where so many had died or were dying. Opponents of the theater circulated a black-bordered handbill through the ghetto: "One does not present shows in cemeteries."[11]

Perhaps not, replied the theater people, but one doesn't quit living while yet alive either. On January 18, 1942, the ghetto theater presented its first performance to an audience of councilmen, policemen, and their families. The program was restrained and dignified, in keeping with the seriousness of the times. The theater eventually won acceptance, and was well-attended until the ghetto's last, tragic days.

## "Even Here, Reason for Rejoicing"

*Simchas* ("joyous events") have always played an important role in Jewish life, marking the passage of time and the changing of the seasons. In the ghetto, one never knew about the next year, so it was important to celebrate to the full in the here and now. People marked birthdays, anniversaries and weddings, finding some measure of joy in the small landmarks of life.

When longtime widower Chaim Rumkowski announced that he planned to get married, everyone in the ghetto wanted to know who she was, how they met, where they would

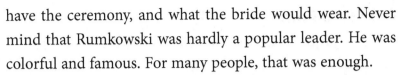

have the ceremony, and what the bride would wear. Never mind that Rumkowski was hardly a popular leader. He was colorful and famous. For many people, that was enough.

"Probably no wireless telegraph in the world ever functioned as efficiently and swiftly . . . as the ghetto's 'whispering telegraph,'" gushed a contributor to the Lodz ghetto chronicle. The news traveled by word of mouth on the streets, in the lines, in the stores . . . in a matter of seconds it was all over town."[12]

Rumkowski's bride, Regina Weinberger, was an attorney nearly thirty years his junior. They were married in a small ceremony at the groom's apartment. For Rumkowski to take such a bold, life-affirming step gave the people new hope for their own survival.

Like personal occasions, religious holidays played a vital role in strengthening people to face the daily challenges of survival. Many Jewish holidays have a theme of liberation from tyranny or deliverance from destruction, messages that the ghettos needed to hear. Hanukkah commemorates the legendary Maccabees and their fight for religious freedom in 168 B.C.; Passover tells of Moses leading his people out of slavery in Egypt. Both are luminous, joyous, yet ultimately reverent.

Purim has a different kind of joy; playful at times, even rowdy. It centers around the biblical story of Esther, the beautiful queen who outwitted the wicked Haman and foiled his plot to kill all the Jews of Persia. This rollicking celebration of danger averted and enemies destroyed had special meaning for Jews living in the shadow of Nazi terror.

## A Special Purim

Even under the Nazi shadow, the Jews of the Kovno ghetto managed to put together a memorable Purim celebration. The Nazis tried to ruin it by declaring a day of mourning for their fallen war heroes. In recognition of this solemn occasion, the Nazis banned all public displays of rejoicing or merrymaking.

The Jews of the Kovno ghetto decided to ignore that order. The children had spent weeks rehearsing a play; the women had scraped together ingredients for the traditional pastries known as *Hamantaschen* ("Haman's ears"); everything was ready. The Jews gathered at a hall deep in the ghetto, where the Germans weren't likely to notice them.

The children put on their play for an audience of misty-eyed parents and ghetto dignitaries. Avraham Tory described this brave performance in his journal:

> A boy named Reuben mounted the stage; he [wore] royal robes, with a crown on his head. . . . 'I am King Ahasuerus,' [he said] and seated himself on the throne. Then [came] Shulamit—a pretty . . . six-year-old . . . wearing a pink dress and a jewel-studded crown. . . . This, of course, was Queen Esther in full splendor. She bowed to King Ahasuerus and to the audience. Then the other members of the troupe mounted the stage. . . . Little charming Shulamit, leading all the dancers, was the audience's favorite.[13]

Everyone had a fine time. The audience cheered Esther and her elderly protector Mordecai. They booed lustily and whirled their *greigers* (noisemakers) whenever Haman appeared. After the program, people shared the meager refreshments and made small talk. A hundred Jewish children ran free, laughing, teasing, chasing, occasionally

shoving; in other words, acting like ordinary children. German orders notwithstanding, the people of Kovno transformed that particular Purim into one of those all-too-brief moments of brightness that helped to make ghetto life more bearable.

# MATTERS OF LIFE AND DEATH

On June 22, 1941, Nazi troops invaded the Soviet Union in what came to be called Operation Barbarossa, after the medieval king Frederick I, who was nicknamed Barbarossa (red beard). This assault represented what Holocaust historian Martin Gilbert described as "a tragic turning-point in German policy towards the Jews."[1]

Soviet troops gave way under the onslaught, and thousands of Russian Jews fell into enemy hands. In the cities, the Nazis set up ghettos as they had done in Poland: Minsk, Bialystok, Vilna, Kiev. In the countryside, they did not bother deporting Jews; they rounded them up and killed them on the spot. During the first five weeks of Operation Barbarossa, the Nazis killed more Jews than they had killed in the previous eight years.[2]

## The Killing Squads

Behind the tanks and troops and cannons of war came the *Einsatzgruppen* (mobile killing units). Formed by Reinhard Heydrich, whose order had created the ghettos, these rear-guard units had one purpose: to kill Jews. Four squads, designated A through D, followed a set procedure when they swept through a newly conquered area. Once the sweep began, the unit would enter a town and order all Jews to assemble for resettlement: "They were requested to hand over their valuables . . . and shortly before the execution to surrender their outer clothing," said Otto Ohlendorf, commander of Einsatzgruppe D. "The men, women, and children were led to a place of execution which in most cases was located next to a more deeply excavated anti-tank ditch. Then they were shot, kneeling or standing, and the corpses were thrown into the ditch."[3]

When asked how many Jews his group had killed in this manner, Ohlendorf answered promptly, "Ninety thousand!" This was one squad, over a single twelve-month period. The Einsatzgruppen lasted for almost two years; no one knows exactly how many Jews they killed, but estimates run as high as 2 million.[4]

In cities with large Jewish populations, the Nazis turned killing into a science. Wherever possible, they found a site that could be specially adapted to their murderous purposes. Ponar, Babi Yar, Ninth Fort—these were some of the killing places, each one near enough to a major city to be accessible, but far enough away to be "discreet."

Vilna was a main target for the Einsatzgruppen, perhaps because Jews accounted for one third of the city's population. When the Germans took the city, fifty-seven thousand Jews lived there. Six months later, only twenty thousand remained alive.[5] The rest were killed in the woods of Ponar, twelve kilometers outside the city.

The Germans sent people to Ponar by the truckload, claiming they were bound for a concentration camp. Abba Kovner, who later became a leader in the Jewish underground, was among the first to realize that the "concentration camp" was a ruse. On December 31, 1941, he issued a proclamation to an assembly of Jewish youth: "Ponar is not a concentration camp. [The deported Jews] have all been shot there. Hitler plans to destroy all the Jews of Europe, and the Jews of Lithuania have been chosen as the first in line."[6] Kovner called upon the Jews of Vilna to fight; but only a few were willing to believe he was right about the mass murders. Such a thing would be too terrible, even for Nazis.

The Jews of Kiev in the Ukraine faced similar horror at a ravine called Babi Yar. Over two days at the end of September 1941, it became the site of the largest single shooting massacre of the Holocaust.[7] On September 29 and 30, posters all over the city called Jews to assemble for "resettlement." More than thirty-three thousand obeyed the order, and were promptly taken to Babi Yar to be killed and cast into the ravine.

In Kovno, the place of death was Ninth Fort, one of a series of forts ringing the city. The forts protected Kovno from invasion during war, and in times of peace served as maximum-security prisons. Ninth Fort was close to the Kovno ghetto, so the Germans used it for imprisoning and killing thousands of Jews.

The Kovno ghetto was divided into two sections, known simply as the "big ghetto" and the "small ghetto." In October

1941, German policemen and Lithuanian collaborators broke into the small ghetto and began driving Jews out of their homes. Assemble in the street and line up in marching columns, the policemen yelled. The Jews did as they were told, too stunned to do otherwise. Avraham Tory called it "a procession of mourners grieving over themselves."[8]

## Big Lies, Unbelievable Truths

In their quest for more "efficient" methods of killing, the Einsatzgruppen began using poison gas instead of machine guns to kill their victims. Engineers trans-formed ordinary covered trucks into portable gas chambers. Unsuspecting prisoners boarded the trucks for a journey to a "new location." What they found was death. The driver simply started the engine and floored the accelerator, pumping lethal exhaust into the sealed truck. Fifteen minutes later, everyone inside was dead.

While Soviet Jews died in vast massacres, Polish Jews were still trying to survive in their ghettos. They did not realize yet that the threat that had hung over them for so long was actually a death sentence from which there was no appeal. They remained trapped between their own inability to believe the unbelievable and the Nazi talent for deception. Chaim Rumkowski told the people of Lodz that work had made them safe. Never mind the rumors, he said. So long as the Nazis needed what the ghetto could produce, Jewish workers would survive. He, Mordecai Chaim Rumkowski, would see to that.

Adam Czerniakow of Warsaw was neither so trusting nor so confident of his own ability to "save" anyone. Although a growing sense of doom weighed on him as conditions worsened, he could not bring himself to believe that Jews chosen for "resettlement" were in fact going to their deaths. Such a thing seemed too monstrous to be true.

Adolf Hitler was a master of big, monstrous lies: "The size of the lie is a definite factor in causing it to be believed," he once said.

> The vast masses of the nation are in the depths of their hearts more easily deceived than they are consciously and intentionally bad. The primitive simplicity of their minds renders them a more easy prey to a big lie than a small one, for they themselves often tell little lies but would be ashamed to tell a big one.[9]

Again and again in the short, bloody history of the ghettos, the Nazis tricked Jews into acting against their own best interests. Mark Gotfried, the teacher whose selections for the Tarnopol ghetto council were executed on the spot, was not the only person victimized by this ruse. By the summer and early autumn of 1942, the Nazis had used this deception in one ghetto after another and one situation after another.

## Choosing When to Die

For many desperate people, suicide became the ultimate act of defiance. Though Jewish tradition affirms the sanctity of life, Jewish history acknowledges times when suicide is acceptable, as a form of *kiddush hashem*.

In A.D. 70 at the mountain fortress of Masada in Palestine, one thousand Jewish freedom fighters killed themselves rather than surrender to Roman troops. During the Crusades of the Middle Ages, entire Jewish communities committed suicide rather than renounce their faith and accept Christian baptism. In the doomed ghettos of the Holocaust, the only

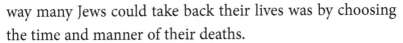

way many Jews could take back their lives was by choosing the time and manner of their deaths.

There were many ways to die in the ghetto. People jumped out of windows, swallowed poison, or hanged themselves. Those with patience simply quit eating and let nature take its course. "Probably the most modern way of [committing suicide]," observed Oskar Singer of Lodz, "is to let oneself be shot by someone duty-bound to do so. . . . In the first days of the ghetto this was very simple. All you had to do was approach the barbed wire and look as if you were about to cross it—and immediately, the liberating shot was fired."[10] This happened so often that people of the ghetto had a name for it: "suicide at the barbed wire."

Some people committed suicide to escape the pain of living. Others did it to escape the pain of dying under Nazi torture. Adam Czerniakow, leader of the Warsaw ghetto, took his own life because he could not bear to take the lives of others.

For two long years, Czerniakow walked a tightrope between cooperation and collaboration. He fully expected to lose his balance one day. That was the reason he kept the cyanide capsules in his desk; to be ready for the order he could not and would not obey. It came on July 22, 1942.

SS Major Hermann Hofle marched into Czerniakow's office and announced that all the Jews of Warsaw were to be deported to the East. Thousands would leave every day; packed into cattle cars, bound for an unnamed destination. Hofle demanded six thousand people that afternoon, assembled at the railroad siding and ready for transport. The next day he wanted more, and that was just the beginning.

This was the "great deportation" Czerniakow had feared for so long. In the past, he had managed to believe that deportees from Warsaw were simply resettled in a new location. He could not believe that any longer. These men, women, and children were not going to work camps; they were going to extermination centers.

Late in the afternoon on July 23, Adam Czerniakow made what was to be his final diary entry: "It is three o'clock. So far, four thousand are ready to go. The orders are that there must be nine thousand by four o'clock."[11]

At four o'clock, he took the cyanide. He died at his desk, leaving nothing but his diary and a note to his wife, containing two short sentences: "[They want] me to kill children with my own hands. There is no other way out and I must die."[12]

## One Family's Tragedy

Calel Perechodnik, the young Jewish policeman who only wanted to "live normally" in spite of the war, saw his life destroyed in a single afternoon. It began on a Wednesday in August 1942, when the SS came to the Otwock ghetto. The officers rode in a limousine; behind them came a troop truck. Soon the sound of gunfire was everywhere in the streets, and the Jews had no place to run.

The survivors were ordered to assemble in the town square on the morning of August 19, 1942. The Jews of Otwock knew what that meant: Hundreds, even thousands, of them would be loaded into cattle cars and shipped to some unknown destination. Most would never return.

Desperate to save his wife and child, Perechodnik sought advice from Commander Kronenberg of the Jewish police.

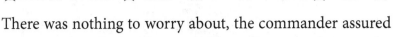

There was nothing to worry about, the commander assured him; policemen's families would be safe. Bring them to the square, and they will be freed after a brief inspection.

Anka Perechodnik did not want to go. There was something suspicious about this amnesty for policemen's families; exactly what she could not say, but something. Perechodnik trusted Kronenberg's assurances and brought his family to the town square.

While they waited to be processed and released, the Jewish police received orders to assemble outside the station. Standing in orderly rows on that hot August day, they listened in dumbfounded misery to the instructions of the Gestapo. They would go through the ghetto, confiscating "abandoned" personal property and disposing of corpses. When the job was completed to the satisfaction of the SS, all policemen would go to the Karczew labor camp to work until the end of the war. The ghetto at Otwock would be no more.

As for wives, the commander's wife and four others who had remained at the station would accompany their husbands to Karczew. Those who went to the square would have to "go away" with the other residents of the ghetto. Too late, Perechodnik realized how skillfully he had been manipulated into betraying his wife and child. Anka Perechodnik and her daughter Athalie were loaded into a cattle car on a train bound for the death camp at Treblinka. Calel would never see them again.

From that terrible day onward, Calel Perechodnik saw his life in a whole new way: "Even if I should survive . . . I cannot live a normal life and look at happy people. I will not remain in Poland, I will not build a new hearth, and I will never be a useful member of society. So what can happen to me? Neither Jew nor Catholic nor a decent man, not even a thief—simply a nobody."[13]

While Perechodnik had watched in helpless horror, another Jewish policeman made a different choice. After the announcement, Abram Willendorf had walked quietly from the police station to the town square. Without a word, he threw aside his policeman's armband, sat down beside his wife and son, and calmly waited for the transport that would take them all to Treblinka.

In the same group with the Willendorfs and his own family, Perechodnik saw the Jew Schussler and his German wife. Although she was *Volksdeutsch* (of pure German blood), she willingly followed her husband of forty years to the ghetto. Now she would follow him to the death camp. Seeing the loyalty of Frau Schussler and Abram Willendorf made Perechodnik feel even worse about his own failure.

## "Our Hands Are Smeared With . . . Blood"

Chaim Rumkowski of Lodz and Jacob Gens of Vilna kept going by convincing themselves that their duty was to ensure that the Jews would survive as a people. This belief led both of them to participate in actions that would horrify most people.

"King Chaim" Rumkowski, the "Eldest of the Jews," began the year 1942 with his usual blustering confidence. Against all evidence to the contrary, he believed that he had great influence with the German commander and that even in Berlin he was well regarded.

When rumors of mass deportations swept through the ghetto, Rumkowski was quick to reassure the people that he was in full control of the ghetto's destiny, and therefore they had nothing to fear: "I don't like to waste words. The stories circulating today are one hundred percent false . . . only those who are, in my opinion, deserving of such a fate will be resettled elsewhere."[14]

After slipping that veiled threat into his monologue, Rumkowski proceeded to brag about his rescue-through-work program, and his own high status with the Germans: "The authorities are full of admiration for the work which has been performed in the ghetto and it is due to that work that they have confidence in me." As proof of this claim, he cited the recent "approval of my motion to reduce the number of deportees from 20,000 to 10,000."[15] If he gave any indication of the grim irony in this "achievement," no one left a record of it.

Nine months later, Rumkowski faced another deportation order, calling for children under ten and adults over sixty-five. This time, he could not talk the Nazis out of their plan.

On September 4, 1942, a stunned Chaim Rumkowski stood before the people of Lodz and told them the news: "We have to accept the evil order. I have to perform this bloody operation myself; I simply must cut off limbs to save the body! I have to take away the children, because otherwise others will also be taken."[16] Rumkowski performed this selection, still convinced in his own mind that he was "saving" Jewish life.

Jacob Gens was less proud and self-important than Rumkowski, though equally "realistic" in his decisions: "It is true that our hands are smeared with the blood of our brethren, but we had to accept this horrible task," he once told the Jews of Vilna. "It is our duty to save the strong and the young and not let sentiment overcome us. . . . I personally take responsibility for all that has happened. I don't want any discussion. I have called you to explain why a Jew dips his hands in blood . . ."[17]

Gens made this speech a few days after deporting four hundred elderly Jews in order to save six hundred younger ones. By this time, he surely knew the fate of the deportees. He could not hide behind the convenient fiction of "resettlement" to ease his conscience or justify himself to the Jewish community. Still, he made the selections, and still he sent Jewish police to track down those who failed to appear.

Militant young Jews began to realize something that the older generations could not bring themselves to believe: The Nazis actually meant to wipe the Jewish people from the face of the earth. It was time to fight, they said; but the councils believed that resistance would lead to the utter destruction of the ghettos.

Many younger Jews fled the ghettos to organize an underground, a secret fighting unit. Some slipped out under cover of darkness; others bribed their way past checkpoints or used false identification papers. Many of them linked up with Jews who had taken refuge in the forests of central Europe and the Soviet Union.

# LIVING IN THE CRACKS

While the Jewish leadership tried to satisfy Nazi demands in order to save the ghettos, ordinary Jews were busy simply trying to survive from one day to the next. To preserve their last shred of freedom, Jews learned how to hide from Jewish police and Nazi soldiers, how to pose as Gentiles on the Aryan side, how to steal and how to smuggle. Some even became outlaws and gangsters.

## The Smugglers

Smuggling was not only common in the ghettos, but necessary for survival. Ghetto food rations were calculated for slow starvation. Knowing the need for adequate food, most Jewish councils tolerated smuggling, or even encouraged it. According to estimates in the Warsaw ghetto, legal imports accounted for two million zlotys; illegal ones, for as much as eighty million zlotys.[1]

Emmanuel Ringelblum tells of two men known throughout the Warsaw ghetto as Kohn and Heller. Before the war, they operated a successful import-export business. During the war, they secretly turned to large-scale smuggling. Kohn and Heller brought in huge quantities of food and medicine, maintained a retail food store within the ghetto, and operated horse-drawn streetcars that provided the ghetto's only form of public transportation. In their spare time, they blackmailed ghetto residents and acted as informers for the Germans.

Another Jewish criminal, Abraham Gancwajch, managed to get appointed director of a special "economic police force" in the Warsaw ghetto. Under direct orders from the Gestapo, Gancwajch and his henchmen set up an office at 13 Leszno Street. Because of this address, the organization quickly became known as "the Thirteen." Its job was to mount a "war against speculation and excessive prices"[2]; in other words, to crack down on smuggling and black market activities.

The Thirteen soon had a hand in every illegal enterprise within the ghetto. They ran a "protection" racket, taking huge payoffs from people who were involved in the selling, buying, or transporting of illegal goods. At one time, Gancwajch had become so powerful that he challenged Adam Czerniakow and the Judenrat for control of the ghetto government. His "reign" ended abruptly in 1942, when the Gestapo swept through the ghetto, killing every member of the Thirteen they could find. Gancwajch himself slipped through their net. He was never seen again.

Most smugglers were not highly organized professionals, but ordinary people who transported small quantities of

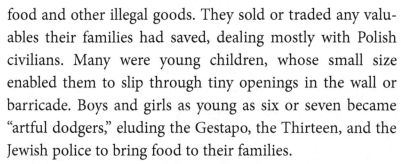

food and other illegal goods. They sold or traded any valuables their families had saved, dealing mostly with Polish civilians. Many were young children, whose small size enabled them to slip through tiny openings in the wall or barricade. Boys and girls as young as six or seven became "artful dodgers," eluding the Gestapo, the Thirteen, and the Jewish police to bring food to their families.

"All of them bear humps on their backs . . .," Chaim Kaplan observed. "Anyone who didn't know their occupation would think them deformed."[3] The humps were actually storage containers, filled with potatoes, onions, and any other foods the youngsters had managed to obtain.

## The Secret People

Smugglers weren't the only ones who slipped past the Nazis. Many people survived by hiding inside the ghetto during resettlement actions and at other times of crisis. A good hideout was especially necessary for those who were candidates for deportation because of age, physical condition, or lack of work skills.

Chaim Kaplan in Warsaw fell into this category of "expendable" Jews; he had no job and no money for bribes and payoffs. "My only salvation is in hiding," he wrote. "This is an outlaw's life, and a man cannot last very long living illegally."[4]

When troops came to take people to forced labor camps or the dreaded resettlements, a hideaway could make the difference between living and dying. Even a hasty evacuation to the cellar could save lives. The authorities could not search every nook and cranny in the ghetto. Some would slip through their net.

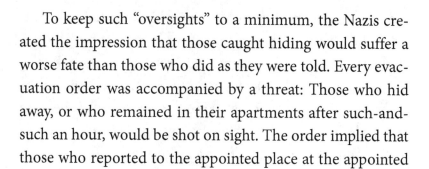

To keep such "oversights" to a minimum, the Nazis created the impression that those caught hiding would suffer a worse fate than those who did as they were told. Every evacuation order was accompanied by a threat: Those who hid away, or who remained in their apartments after such-and-such an hour, would be shot on sight. The order implied that those who reported to the appointed place at the appointed time would be dealt with fairly.

Some saw through the ruse and hid anyway. In an emergency, they used all kinds of hideouts: behind furniture, under beds, in dumbwaiters, garrets, and air raid shelters—any place they thought the Nazis might not look. Their safety could be destroyed instantly by a crying child or an accidental cough. Jewish policemen often specialized in ferreting out hiding places. Emmanuel Ringelblum estimated that these police betrayed thousands of their own people to the authorities.[5]

As the occupation wore on, even the most determined optimists realized their mortal danger. They began to design clever, well-concealed hideouts. The Jurman family of the Buczacz ghetto concealed themselves inside a stone wall in their backyard. The wall was built against a hillside, with a surprising amount of space inside. They worked out a way to remove three large stones and replace them from inside, using a makeshift wooden frame to keep them in place. The result looked like any other retaining wall against any other hill in that part of Poland.

The hillside hideout worked nicely through the summer and early autumn, then the family needed another plan: "Winter was coming, and it would not be safe to use . . . the

"backyard wall again," recalled Alicia Jurman, who was twelve years old at the time.

> The heavy rains might wash away the soil we put between the removable stones, and anyone . . . would be able to detect the irregularity between the stones. . . . We worked many nights building our new bunker. . . . The opening . . . was under the big brick oven in which there were two small doors that normally opened to the firewood bin. We removed the wooden floor of the bin and dug a tunnel about ten feet under the hall in order to avoid the sound of hollowness.[6]

A large storage box covered the entrance.

By late 1942, hideout design and construction had become an important industry in the Warsaw ghetto. The people of the ghetto were coming to realize that the latest "resettlement" would not be the last, no matter what the Germans said. There was always another transport, always another lie. Anyone who hoped to survive needed a refuge where they could be completely self-sufficient for weeks, even months at a time.

People stocked their shelters with preserved food and equipped them with modern conveniences such as gas, electricity, and running water. The most imaginative of the fugitives had contingency plans for everything: candles and kerosene lanterns in case the electricity went out; piles of woolen blankets to tide them over through a lack of heat; barrels of distilled water in case service should be cut off at the main valve.

In the event that the emergency water supply ran out, some imaginative fugitives developed what Emmanuel Ringelblum called a brilliant scheme for obtaining water. They would sneak outside under the cover of darkness and set fire to an empty house. When firefighters came clanging to the rescue, the first thing they did was open the water mains. While the fire was being fought, the hidden Jews would replenish their water supplies.[7]

In the Kovno ghetto, Avraham Tory was running out of places to hide. People were being transferred to SS labor camps, and what remained of the ghetto became a concentration camp. Dr. Elkhanan Elkes, a friend who knew about Tory's diary, told him to get out of the ghetto while he still had time: Protect the diary at all costs; people had to know what had happened here.

With the help of the underground, Tory slipped out of the ghetto and joined his friend Pnina Sheinzon and her daughter Shulamit, the delicate little dancer of the Purim play. They had been living some miles from the city, sheltered by sympathetic Lithuanian farmers. For four months, Tory lived in an isolated hut, eating what his Lithuanian friends were able to bring him, and fearing any unfamiliar sound.

## The False "Aryans"

People who looked "Aryan" could sometimes escape the ghetto by posing as Gentiles. Living on "the other side" was risky business. The smallest gesture or misspoken word could undo everything: a Yiddish lilt in the voice, an awkwardness in making the sign of the cross, or a puzzling ignorance about how to behave at church.

Calel Perechodnik's father felt certain that he was equal to the challenge of "passing." He lived as a Gentile, convinced that his Polish-Catholic identity papers would see him through every danger. As the only one in the family with the papers and the appearance to pose as a Gentile, Oszer

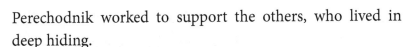

Perechodnik worked to support the others, who lived in deep hiding.

Although he was familiar with the manners and customs of the country, his masquerade ultimately failed. He got home one night to find a pair of German guards standing at his front door. The pretense was over, they said; an anonymous informant had denounced him as a Jew. They dragged Oszer away that night; no one ever heard from him again.

Many Jews who could not get out of the ghetto themselves arranged to send their children to safety with Christian families. Sympathetic priests assured the parents that their children would not be converted, but they would need to behave like Christians for the safety of all concerned. Many a frightened Jewish child went though a crash course on kneeling, praying, and making the sign of the cross.

Babies presented a special challenge for the foster parents. They had to raise the child as a Christian to avoid suspicion, but they were honor-bound to return him or her to Jewish parents when the danger had passed. When Josef Jachowicz and his wife took two-year-old Shachne Hiller into their home, they fell in love with his bright eyes and quick mind.

Mrs. Jachowicz took him to church regularly, delighted at the way he memorized the Sunday hymns. When she learned that his parents died in the liquidation of the Krakow ghetto, Mrs. Jachowicz took the baby to her parish priest. Shachne was born Jewish, she told Father Karol Wojtyla, but now his parents were dead. She wanted to have the child baptized and raise him as the Christian son of Christian parents.

The young priest refused to perform the sacrament. He reminded the Jachowiczes that they had promised to tell

Shachne of his Jewish origins and return him to his people if the Hillers did not survive the war. They were honor-bound to fulfill that promise.

With the help of his Polish foster parents, Shachne Hiller survived the war and was sent to live with relatives in the United States. The priest who convinced Mrs. Jachowicz to honor her promise went on to become Pope John Paul II.[8]

## The Odyssey of Alicia Jurman

Not all children were so carefully sheltered, or so well prepared for their Christian identities. Twelve-year-old Alicia Jurman had to make the adjustment entirely on her own after escaping from the very edge of a mass grave. Separated from her family during the liquidation of Buczacz ghetto, Alicia found herself in a prison where hundreds of Jews were packed into a courtyard without food, water, or sanitary facilities.

They were held there overnight, and the next morning marched to a meadow where a large trench cut across the ground like a jagged brown scar. Not until the soldiers started shooting did Alicia realize the full horror of her situation. This was a mass execution; the trench was a grave that would soon be filled with row upon row of Jewish bodies. "As I was nearing the pit," Alicia remembered, "I thought I heard my name being called. . . . 'Alicia—Alicia Jurman!' All of a sudden we heard machine-gun fire . . . I turned my head to see what was happening and saw Milek [a friend from Buczacz] . . . holding a machine gun . . . and shooting at the Germans. 'Alicia, run! Get out of here! Run!' Milek was calling as he kept shooting at the Germans."[9]

Alicia ran, and kept running until she dropped from pure exhaustion. She slept where she fell, and in the morning she began working her way back toward Buczacz ghetto. Her family had agreed to meet there if they got separated from one another.

To support herself, Alicia pretended to be a Christian peasant girl, trading work for food at farms along the way: "With my hair braided and [wearing a] bandanna I looked like a typical peasant girl, Polish or Ukrainian. I tried to imitate the free, swaying walk of the village girls and was able to do so because my feet had become callused enough to step freely on the hard earth."[10]

The road home proved to be an excellent "laboratory" for practicing the fine arts of masquerade and survival. Alicia traveled through an area populated by both Ukrainians and Poles. These two very similar peoples hated one another, so Alicia needed two false identities. To Poles, she introduced herself as "Helka" and to Ukrainians, as "Slavka." She developed a clever test for deciding which name to use: The Poles were Roman Catholics and the Ukrainians, Greek Orthodox. The standard greeting in both languages was "Praised be Jesus Christ" and the response would be "Forever and ever, Amen." Polish and Ukrainian are very similar languages. "I decided to mumble the greetings. The listener really could not tell which language I was using. I would listen carefully for the reply and then use whichever language I heard."[11]

Not only did Alicia find her mother, she kept the two of them a step ahead of the Gestapo. She also helped rescue other Jews from doomed ghettos and compromised hideouts. When people were hungry, she found them food; when they were sick, she found them medicine.

Living in the cracks of a society gone mad had its price. It cost Alicia Jurman her childhood; almost overnight, she became an adult with a finely honed sense of survival. The "price" was different for every survivor; truthful people learned to lie, honest ones to evade the law. Regardless of how they coped, all survivors had this in common: They did things they never thought they would do, and were forever changed by the experience.

## Chapter 6

# LEGACIES OF COURAGE

In the ghettos, courage took different forms. For activists, courage meant armed resistance, fighting for honor, even when there was no chance of winning. Those who were too old, too young, or too weak to fight endured whatever came their way without surrendering their moral scruples or human dignity.

## The Quiet Heroes

The stubborn courage of ordinary Jews could not be entirely crushed by ghettos and gas chambers. Rabbi Mosze Friedman was one of these quiet heroes. Transported from the ghetto to Auschwitz, he called up his last strength for an act of moral resistance that left even the Nazis stunned.

Stripped of his clothing, waiting to die, Rabbi Friedman grabbed a startled SS lieutenant by the lapels and gave him a proper dressing-down: "You common, cruel murderers of mankind, do not think you will succeed in extinguishing our nation. . . ."[1] When he finished speaking, the rabbi clapped his hat onto his head and shouted in a strong, clear voice: "*Shema Israel!*" ("Hear, O Israel"). "*Shema Israel!*" replied the Jews, all of them naked as the rabbi himself, and soon to die: "*Shema Israel, Adonai Elohenu, Adonai e'chad*"—("Hear O Israel, the Lord is our God, the Lord is One")—the ancient affirmation of faith that comforts Jews in times of adversity and consoles them at the hour of death.

Even young children could display this kind of defiant courage. At the Orphaned Child's Home in Warsaw, Polish director Janusz Korczak helped his young Jewish charges face deportation. When the Nazis came to take them away, all two hundred children stood quietly, dressed and ready for their "journey." Standing in front of them was Janusz Korczak:

> Bareheaded, he led the way, holding a child by each hand. Behind him were the rest of the two hundred children and a group of nurses clad in white aprons. . . . One could see how weak and undernourished the children were. But they marched to their deaths in exemplary order, without a single tear, in such a terrifying silence that it thundered with indictment and defiance.[2]

Sometimes in a crisis, even a villain would find it within himself to behave like a hero. Such was the case of a Judenrat member known only as M.R. in the survivor testimonies that were collected after the war. In Opoczno ghetto, he was the man to see if any Jew landed in a Gestapo jail. The Germans listened to M.R. as they listened to no other Jew in Opoczno, especially when he brought them large cash "gifts." Whenever desperate families gave him money for bribes, a good chunk of it seemed to end up in his own pocket.

M.R. made his living from the pain of others. Until June 1942, he behaved like a man who had no regrets. Then twenty young Jews were arrested for escaping their forced labor brigade. As he had done many times before, M.R. interceded on their behalf; but this time, nobody was listening. This time, the offenders would be executed as a public example of the price of resistance.

No one knows why M.R. rebelled against this particular injustice, but he warned the prisoners of their fate. That night they escaped, and M.R. went into hiding rather than help the Germans track them down. The commandant invoked collective responsibility, threatening to kill one hundred Jews if M.R. did not return. To everyone's surprise, the infamous collaborator of Opoczno surrendered. "What took place then is not known," said a survivor in his report. "However, [M]R.'s dead body was found in the hall of the German [headquarters]. Thus, the former informant died a hero's death."[3]

## Fighting Back

When the deportations from the Warsaw ghetto finally came to an end, a population that once numbered 350,000 had been reduced to less than 35,000. Those left behind knew that their own days were also numbered. The time would come when their only choice would be when and how they would die.

Hopelessness made them bold; if they could do nothing to change their fate, then it would be both cowardice and stupidity to continue bargaining with the Germans for their lives. It would be better to go down fighting: "Most of the populace is set on resistance," wrote Emmanuel Ringelblum.

"It seems to me that people will no longer go to the slaughter like lambs. . . . Whomever you talk to, you hear the same cry. . . . We must put up a resistance, defend ourselves against the enemy, man and child."[4]

Even during the deportations, a group of young Jews gathered in secret on July 28, 1942, to assemble the nucleus of the Jewish Fighting Organization (Zydowska Organizacja Bojowa [ZOB]). Among the first members of the group were Itzak ("Antek") Zuckerman and Zivia Lubetkin, two people who were destined to achieve legendary status among ghetto fighters.

Both were realists; they did not expect to defeat a vastly superior force. They did expect to make a resounding statement on behalf of all the murdered Jews: "This small group [the ZOB] still has the strength to restore our honor," wrote Zuckerman of those days in early September 1942. "We will be killed. It is fitting that we should be killed. But our honor will be victorious. There will be a day when we are remembered: the youth of this helpless people have risen and saved our honor with everything they had."[5]

News of the deportations, and probably of the resistance, reached Warsaw-born Mordecai Anielewicz in eastern Poland. He left his work with the underground to join the Jews of Warsaw. Anielewicz was twenty-two years old, a natural leader with a burning desire to strike a punishing blow against the Nazis.

He helped to unite Jews from many different youth groups and political persuasions into a unified force. Under his leadership, the ZOB began putting together a weapons arsenal, preparing for battle. Members trained in secret,

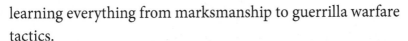

learning everything from marksmanship to guerrilla warfare tactics.

The first ZOB missions targeted the most notorious collaborators in the Jewish administration, beginning with attorney Jakub Lejkin, deputy commander of the Jewish police. It was Lejkin who orchestrated the deportations that had decimated the Warsaw ghetto. He was coldly efficient in this work, showing no mercy for the victims and no regret for his crimes.

The ZOB sentenced him to death, and on October 29, 1942, three members of the underground carried out that sentence. The ZOB posted notices all over the ghetto, informing the public that Lejkin had been executed for crimes against the Jewish people. A few days later, Judenrat member Yisrael First was executed for his activities as an informer. These judgments sent shock waves through the ghetto. Collaborators who once swaggered with pride in their secondhand power began to watch their backs.

## On the Other Side of the Wall

To obtain arms and ammunition, as well as other forms of help for their planned rebellion, the ZOB sent "Aryan-looking" members to the Polish side of Warsaw. One of these agents was nineteen-year-old Feigele Peltel; in addition to her "Aryan" appearance, Peltel spoke fluent Polish and knew how to think on her feet. In the days to come, those qualities would be the difference between life and death.

Her plan to escape the ghetto was simple enough, but far from safe. She would march out, in full view of Jewish police and German guards, as part of a labor brigade going to work on the "Aryan" side. In her memoirs published under her nickname and married name, Vladka Meed, Peltel recalled that chilly December morning in 1942: "At 7:00 A.M. the street was astir with people streaming to work. . . . After some searching, I found a Jewish leader of a forty-man labor battalion who for 500 zlotys allowed me to join his group."[6]

Even on this first trip, Peltel did not go empty-handed. She carried an underground communiqué containing vital information about the Treblinka extermination camp. On the advice of her roommates in the ghetto, she had folded the document and placed it in her shoe.

As the only woman in her group, Peltel attracted the attention of a German guard, who singled her out for a thorough search. "I found myself in a dimly lit room, its blood-spattered walls papered with maps, charts, and photographs of half-naked women," Peltel recalled. "I stood by the wall and waited . . . [fighting] for control over the terror that seemed about to engulf me."[7]

By the sheerest stroke of luck, the guard who searched Peltel was called away before he could check her shoes. She dressed quickly and hurried outside, trying to look as if everything was in good order. When a sentry asked where she was going, Peltel faced him with outward calm: "To the labor battalion . . . I have already passed inspection."[8] He hesitated for a moment, then waved her through.

Once on the Aryan side, Peltel removed the armband that identified her as a Jew, and "Feigele" became "Vladka," complete with false identity papers, obtained with the help of Christian friends, and a daytime job as a seamstress.

## The January "Action"

On January 18, 1943, at six o'clock in the morning, the next round-up of Jews from Warsaw began. The Nazis proceeded in the usual way: German troops, assisted by a detachment of well-armed Ukrainian collaborators, stomped through the ghetto streets at 6:00 A.M., ordering Jews to assemble in their courtyards. They raided the assembly points where workers waited to go to their jobs.

Those they captured were treated mercilessly, bullied and beaten, marched to the railroad track, and packed into box-cars like sardines in a can. A number of Judenrat members were seized that day, along with their families. In just a few hours, the Germans took five thousand people.[9] All of them went straight to the gas chambers of Treblinka.

By striking hard and fast, the Nazis had caught the ZOB unaware. There was no time to plan strategies or even assemble into armed companies. Mordecai Anielewicz had to improvise. He devised a simple plan to disrupt the round-up: Twelve fighters with concealed pistols would infiltrate the lines of Jews bound for the death trains. At a signal, they would attack the German guards, giving at least some of the captured Jews a chance to flee.

All twelve volunteers expected to die in this attack against a vastly superior force, but that did not stop them from doing what had to be done. They fell into the line, spacing themselves for as much strategic advantage as possible. At the signal, each fighter attacked the nearest guard. The fierceness and outright audacity of this operation shocked the Germans. Before they could react or call up reserves, hundreds of captive Jews had fled for cover, and the

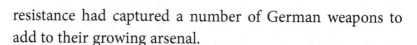

resistance had captured a number of German weapons to add to their growing arsenal.

Only two freedom fighters survived that mission, but they had freed many doomed Jews and inflicted casualties on the Germans. Jews had killed Germans in combat. This had never happened before, and it changed things in the ghetto. The Jews became braver and more reckless; the Germans were more careful as they faced the prospect of armed enemies who could strike from the shadows of an alleyway or stand waiting behind an apartment door. The deportations stopped for the time being, as the Nazis pulled back to figure out how to deal with this unexpected development.

"The ghetto was proud of this event," wrote Vladka Meed. "'They panicked,' the Jews told each other gleefully, going over the details again and again. Yet it was clear that the Germans would return, that they would relentlessly pursue their objective of making Warsaw judenrein [empty of Jews]."[10]

## "Get Us Weapons!"

The January revolt was a benchmark event in the life of the ghetto. After the dust settled and the Germans left, nothing was the same. The ZOB no longer had to wonder if the ghetto was ready to make a stand. Even the Judenrat supported the resistance. When the Germans asked council president Marc Lichtenbaum to calm the situation among the Jewish workers, he told them flatly that there was nothing he could do: "I am not the authority in the ghetto," he said. "There is another authority—the Jewish Fighting Organization."[11]

The Jews were ready to fight, but Mordecai Anielewicz and the other underground leaders knew that courage and a

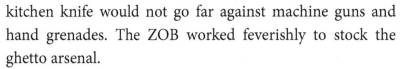

kitchen knife would not go far against machine guns and hand grenades. The ZOB worked feverishly to stock the ghetto arsenal.

The Polish underground sent about forty-nine pistols and a small number of grenades; Jewish operatives on the Aryan side bought guns from anyone willing to sell; and one young resistance fighter convinced an explosives expert to help him create the bombs-in-a-bottle known as "Molotov cocktails."

Soon underground members on the Aryan side were smuggling chemicals to secret munitions factories inside the ghetto. "It was difficult to get the gasoline, acid, and potash we needed," wrote Vladka Meed. "We purchased the 'merchandise' from . . . various parts of the city, and occasionally . . . [transported] the ingredients across Warsaw by horse-cart. If we were discovered, it would mean death. Until they could be smuggled into the ghetto, the . . . chemicals were hidden under our own beds."[12]

From the Nazi point of view, the January uprising had set a dangerous precedent. If Jews all over the occupied territories began to fight instead of going meekly to their deaths, they could drain much-needed resources from the war effort. The Nazis had no intention of letting that happen.

The war effort needed all the help it could get. Since the beginning of Operation Barbarossa, resistance in the east had stiffened. On February 2, 1943, at Stalingrad in the Soviet Union, Germany suffered the worst defeat in its military history. Almost overnight, the situation on the eastern front began to come apart. Now it was the Soviet army advancing, pushing the Nazis back.

Despite this reversal of fortune, Hitler refused to divert men and materials from his war against the Jews. He wanted more troops, more trains, more gas chambers and crematoria. The pace and brutality of "actions" and "resettlements" increased at an alarming rate.

## Under Siege

The Warsaw ghetto soon felt the effects of Hitler's determination. On April 19, 1943, SS General Jurgen Stroop led an all-out assault against the ghetto. More than two thousand German troops armed with machine guns and field artillery surrounded the ghetto. The ZOB had half the manpower, no artillery, and only two machine guns. The rest of their weaponry consisted of seventeen rifles, five hundred pistols, and an undetermined quantity of grenades and homemade bombs.[13] At the onset of the fighting, Mordecai Anielewicz found an unexpected hiding place for his headquarters: a bunker at 18 Mila Street, deep in the ghetto. Zivia Lubetkin wrote:

> This bunker belonged to the members of Warsaw's Jewish underworld. They had dug a large shelter deep into the earth underneath a block of three huge buildings which had been destroyed in September, 1939. A narrow passageway cut through the bunker and the ample shelter, with its many rooms, electricity, running water, kitchen, bedroom, and even a living room.[14]

From this base and others scattered throughout the ghetto, the Jews went out to engage the enemy. They fought from alleyways and rooftops, relying upon concealment and surprise to harass the enemy. Gunfire came from "empty" windows; Molotov cocktails and grenades exploded all around. The Jewish fighters struck quickly and disappeared, often before the enemy even knew they were there. "When the Germans came up to our posts and marched by and we threw those hand grenades and bombs . . . there was rejoicing," said ZOB fighter Zivia Lubetkin. "The tomorrow did not worry us."[15]

The next day, the Germans began shelling the buildings and setting fire to anything that would burn. The ZOB fighters raced along the rooflines and through garrets, keeping pace with the German advance. Flames engulfed so much of the ghetto that people could see the fire and rising smoke from miles around.

On May 8, 1943, German troops discovered the command bunker at 18 Mila Street. After a blazing exchange of gunfire, the Germans flooded the bunker with poison gas. Rather than be captured alive, the Jews turned their guns on themselves. Mordecai Anielewicz and ninety-seven of his comrades died that day. Of the one hundred people in that bunker, only two survived to tell the story.

So it went, day by day; conflagration and wholesale death settled into a macabre routine. "The burning had now gone on for two nightmarish weeks," wrote Vladka Meed. "Some areas had been reduced to smoldering ruins. . . . The Germans marched into the ghetto every morning and each evening at dusk they withdrew. They worked only in broad daylight. They . . . rained incendiaries on the ghetto without letup; the explosions could be heard throughout the city."[16]

As more of the ghetto burned and more of the Jews fell, the survivors marshaled their last strength to resist capture and certain death. Some escaped to the Aryan side or to the forest where partisan groups took them in. The rest were

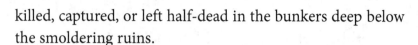

killed, captured, or left half-dead in the bunkers deep below the smoldering ruins.

Zivia Lubetkin and Itzak Zuckerman were among a group of resistance fighters who escaped through the sewers. "It seemed as if you were leaping into the darkness of the depths, with the filthy water splashing and spraying about you," wrote Lubetkin.

> We walk bent and hunched through the slime carrying a candle in one hand. We follow each other in single file. We can't see each other's faces. We feel our way through the darkness and slowly press our way forward. . . . The minutes lag, every hour seems like an eternity. We trudge on for hours with no rest.[17]

By May 16, it was over. The flames could be seen for miles around.

The Warsaw Ghetto, said General Jurgen Stroop, was "no longer in existence."[18]

Even in defeat, the brave young fighters had achieved a great deal. "I feel that great things are happening and that this action which we have dared to take is of enormous value," Mordecai Anielewicz had written on April 23, seventeen days before his death in the bunker at 18 Mila Street. "The last wish of my life has been fulfilled. Jewish self-defense has become a fact. Jewish resistance and revenge have become actualities. I am happy to have been one of the first Jewish fighters in the ghetto."[19]

Reports about how the Warsaw ghetto met its end fascinated Jews everywhere. In the ghettos and the work camps and the forest hideaways, people talked about the astonishing courage of those young fighters, who confronted one of the most powerful armies on earth with pistols and homemade bombs.

## Chapter 7

# THE BEGINNING OF THE END

Jews in many other ghettos tried to organize resistance groups of their own, but there was not much time. The deportations and murders continued into the summer; normal life began to disappear from the remaining ghettos. Many ghettos were already dead; the rest were dying. On July 21, 1943, Gestapo chief Heinrich Himmler made it official, ordering the liquidation of all ghettos in Poland and the Soviet Union.

## Dark Betrayals

When the liquidation order came down, German troops were already retreating before a fierce Soviet counterattack. The alarm passed quickly from one ghetto to the next: The Nazis were no less deadly because they were on the run. As Avraham Tory of the Kovno ghetto put it, "We have no doubts as to who will emerge victorious from this war. At the

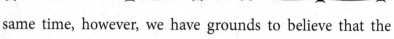

same time, however, we have grounds to believe that the Germans will not be eager to please us by leaving us alive so we can witness their defeat."[1]

In Vilna, Jacob Gens reacted to the increasing danger by trying to tighten his control of the ghetto and show more "cooperation" with the Nazis.

In his diary entry for July 2, 1943, Avraham Tory related a shocking story from Vilna. A Jew was arrested for trying to escape the ghetto and taken to the jail. Terrified of what would happen to him and his family when the authorities discovered he was carrying a gun, the man begged a Jewish policeman to let him go. When the policeman refused, the prisoner shot him to death. Gens promptly took his own gun in hand, marched into the jail and killed the prisoner with a single shot.

Gens was equally ruthless with "troublemakers" whose activities threatened the "security" of the ghetto. Not long after he shot the prisoner in jail, he played a major role in the capture of partisan leader Yitzhak Wittenberg.

The extraordinary sequence of events began on July 8, 1943. Three underground fighters slipped out of the ghetto and blew up a military train on the nearby railroad tracks. The Gestapo was determined to make an example of those responsible for this attack. They arrested and tortured people on the slightest excuse until they finally forced one prisoner to reveal the name of the Jewish resistance leader.

Gens may or may not have aided in Wittenberg's initial capture. Many suspected that he set up a bogus "strategy meeting" to bring Wittenberg out into the open. Whether by accident or design, the result was the same. On the night of

July 16, the Gestapo burst into the Judenrat office and hauled Yitzhak Wittenberg away in chains.

A group of partisans abandoned caution and staged a daring daylight raid. They freed their commander and took him into safe hiding. The Nazis were furious and more determined than ever to make an example of this defiant young Jew.

The Nazis invoked collective responsibility, offering a terrible choice: Hand over Wittenberg, or they would burn the ghetto to the ground. Gens was terrified. "Because of this one man, Wittenberg, the ghetto may be destroyed and annihilated," he told the people.[2] In a mass rally that was more like a riot, hundreds demanded that the partisans deliver their leader to the Nazis.

The standoff between the partisans and those who listened to Gens could have turned into a "civil war," pitting Jew against Jew. Wittenberg refused to let that happen. He appointed Abba Kovner to serve as leader in his place. Then he surrendered voluntarily to the authorities and died a brutal death in the Gestapo jail. Abba Kovner called it "one of the greatest acts of heroism of the Jewish fighting underground."[3] If Gens had regrets about his part in this tragedy, he never spoke of them in public.

In the end, sacrificing Wittenberg did not save the ghetto. Six weeks later, five thousand Jews were deported to labor camps in Estonia. Gens supervised the selections, and when the deportees were gone, he called a meeting of the ten thousand Jews who remained in the ghetto. They came, perhaps expecting words of comfort or defiance. Instead, Gens called upon them to register for work so the ghetto could "return

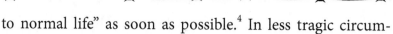

to normal life" as soon as possible.[4] In less tragic circumstances, his words would have been laughable.

Anyone could see that there would never again be "normal life" in the ghetto. Some people escaped to the forests to join the partisans. Some committed suicide. Some were so numbed by horror that they waited for the Nazis to do the job for them. They did not have to wait for long.

On September 14 or 15 (sources differ), Jacob Gens was shot dead in the office of the Gestapo commandant. Less than two weeks later, more than sixteen hundred Jewish men were sent to labor camps in Estonia and Latvia. More than four thousand women, children, and elderly men were shipped to the Majdanek death camp, where they died in vast gas chambers made to look like showers.

Abba Kovner and one hundred of his fighters escaped through the sewers and made their way to the Rudniki Forest. There they continued to fight, harassing the enemy whenever and wherever they could.

By September 25, the Vilna ghetto was no more. Only two thousand slave laborers remained in the area, remnants of a community that once numbered fifty-seven thousand.

## Rude Awakenings

Hayke Grossman of the Bialystok underground risked her life to bring news of the Vilna deportations to Judenrat leader Ephraim Barasz. He assured her that such a thing would never happen in Bialystok. So long as the people were "useful" as workers for the Germans, the ghetto would be safe. "They need us," he said. "Whatever may happen later, we may live in peace for the time being. . . . I shall always know in advance if something is going to happen."[5]

It is unlikely that Hayke Grossman believed these reassurances. As an experienced underground operative, she knew what the Nazis were doing throughout Poland. Relying on her blonde, "non-Jewish" appearance and a set of false identity papers, she smuggled money, goods, and information from one ghetto to another. When a Jewish fugitive needed a place to hide, Grossman would find it. She did what she had to do to help the cause of survival.

Barasz clung to his rescue-through-work idea until the bitter end. He squelched acts of open defiance for fear that the Germans would invoke collective responsibility, punishing the entire ghetto for the actions of a few of its members.

On August 16, 1943, Barasz finally realized that his strategies had failed. At 4:00 A.M. that morning, German soldiers surrounded the Bialystok ghetto. They took over all the factories where Jews had worked as slave laborers and established a base of operations in the Jewish council offices.

In the confusion, many could not decide whether to go into hiding, run to the partisans in the forest, or just wait to see what would happen. Bertha Sokolskaya decided to investigate the situation. "I went to the Judenrat where the [Nazis] . . . were bossing the whole show. Smart, elegant Barasz was trying to ingratiate himself, but . . . they were no longer speaking to him, they were just ordering him about and kicking him."[6]

A handful of young resistance fighters prepared to do battle, Hayke Grossman among them. While they were fighting a short, suicidal battle from makeshift bunkers, Ephraim Barasz was on a train headed for the gas chambers of the Treblinka death camp.

## The Last of Lodz

Chaim Rumkowski's determination to industrialize the Lodz ghetto only postponed its destruction. By mid-1944, the other ghettos were destroyed, the German army was fighting for survival, and the Allies had landed a massive invasion force on the beaches of Normandy. The war, everyone said, would soon be over. Rumkowski kept the remnants of his ghetto busy, perhaps hoping that the Nazis would be so preoccupied with the war that they would "forget" about the Jews of Lodz.

In May 1944, the Nazis asked for three thousand volunteers to clear away debris in the bombed-out city of Munich. A week later, they asked for another three thousand workers to clean up the rubble of yet another German city. Finally, on June 16, they wanted a third group for the same type of work. This last notice said that children who were old enough to work could accompany their parents to the job site.

The Jews of Lodz had learned to be suspicious of all such offers from the Nazis, but these calls for volunteers sounded legitimate. They were specific, they did not make elaborate promises, and they did not try to make the work sound especially easy. All three notices carried the signature of Chaim Rumkowski, Eldest of the Jews of Lodz.

Even at this late date, the Nazis had figured out a new approach to deception. The first two groups of volunteers actually did go to the stated locations and clean up rubble. The third went to the death camp at Chelmno.

The Germans continued the same deception, probably in the interests of speed and "efficiency." On June 23, a new round of deportations began. At the station, the Gestapo commandant assured the Jews that they would be working in the Reich and apologized that the wartime scarcity of equipment made it necessary for them to travel in freight cars. The Nazis even made a great show of transporting people's baggage to the station. Each person was allowed to take hand-luggage along, and "check" larger pieces that would be loaded into the baggage car. It was all very proper and dignified.

Transport after transport followed, always with the same comforting speech. By August, sixty-seven thousand Jews had been deported from the Lodz ghetto to the extermination center at Auschwitz-Birkenau. The crematory ovens burned round the clock, sending plumes of ashes and smoke into the summer sky. Mordecai Chaim Rumkowski and his bride Regina were among the last group taken to the gas chambers.

## Silence and Memories

After the war, on September 18, 1946, searchers going through the ruins of the Warsaw ghetto dug up a group of tin boxes and milk cans that had obviously been buried with some care. Inside, they discovered the first of Emmanuel Ringelblum's Oneg Shabbat histories. Another group of manuscripts was discovered four years later. These papers became known as the Oneg Shabbat Archives.

Ringelblum himself did not survive the war. After the ghetto uprising he found his way to a hideout on the Aryan side. He was captured by the Nazis on March 7, 1944, and executed along with his wife and son. Only his work remains.

The history of the ghettos is ultimately the story of human beings trapped in an inhuman situation. Like human

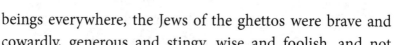

beings everywhere, the Jews of the ghettos were brave and cowardly, generous and stingy, wise and foolish, and not always as noble as they would have liked to have been.

Some, like Calel Perechodnik, were trapped or tricked into betraying everything they loved. They carried an unbearable burden of guilt. Perechodnik never got the chance to find out if he could deal with that guilt; he died of typhus in a hideout on the Aryan side of Warsaw. The last entry in his journal was dated October 9, 1943.

Everyone who lived through those terrible times was in one way or another scarred by the experience. Surviving and building a rewarding life in spite of those scars was in itself an act of courage and an affirmation of life.

Both Abba Kovner of Vilna and Hayke Grossman of Bialystok survived the war and eventually served in the Israeli Knesset (Parliament). Several surviving ghetto fighters married partners who had shared those terrible days and settled in Israel. Zivia Lubetkin and Itzak Zuckerman of Warsaw lived on a kibbutz (collective farm) where they founded the Ghetto Fighters Museum. Avraham Tory and Pnina Sheinzon of Kovno also married and settled in Israel, where they made the remainder of little Shulamit's childhood a happy and normal one. Feigele Peltel, who as Vladka had been an underground agent on the Aryan side of Warsaw, married fellow resistance fighter Benjamin Meed and settled in the United States. Alicia Jurman also went to the United States, where she built a successful career as a writer and teacher.

In a sense, the lives of these survivors are a memorial to the millions of people who perished. Emmanuel Ringelblum was thinking of the slaughtered millions when he praised the

*This copy of a German photograph of women prisoners was taken during the destruction of the Warsaw Ghetto, Poland in 1943.*

"courage of the common Jew" who could not save his own life, but faced his death with quiet dignity and a stubborn refusal to be dehumanized by his murderers.

# CHRONOLOGY

**September 1, 1939**

Germany invades Poland.

**September 5, 1939**

German troops enter Piotrkow.

**September 21, 1939**

Reinhard Heydrich orders the creation of Jewish ghettos.

**October 8, 1939**

First ghetto is established in Piotkrow.

**February 8, 1940**

Lodz ghetto is established.

**May 1, 1940**

Lodz ghetto is sealed.

**October 12, 1940**

"Quarantine" area is established in Warsaw.

**November 15, 1940**

Warsaw ghetto is sealed.

**June 22, 1941**

Operation Barbarossa: Nazis invade Russia.

**June 23, 1941**

Execution squads begin the murder of Russian Jews.

**July 8, 1941**

Mass executions at Ponar.

**July 20, 1941**

Minsk ghetto is established.

**August 1, 1941**

Bialystok ghetto is established.

**September 3–6, 1941**

Vilna ghetto is established.

**September 29–30, 1941**

Kiev Jews are murdered at Babi Yar.

**January 4, 1942**

Rumkowski boasts about "rescue through work."

**January 20, 1942**

Wannsee Conference sets "final solution."

**February 8, 1942**

Beginning of deportations to death camps.

**July 23, 1942**

Suicide of Adam Czerniakow.

**July 28, 1942**

Jewish resistance group is formed in Warsaw.

**September 4, 1942**

Rumkowski deports children of Lodz.

**October 27, 1942**

Gens deports elderly of Vilna.

**January 18, 1943**

Twelve Jewish freedom fighters stage a revolt to disrupt deportation from the Warsaw ghetto.

**February 2, 1943**

Nazis are defeated at Stalingrad.

**April 19, 1943**

Nazis start liquidating the Warsaw ghetto; Warsaw ghetto uprising begins.

**May 16, 1943**

Uprising ends and Warsaw ghetto burns.

**July 21, 1943**

Himmler orders liquidation of all ghettos.

**March 1944**

Emmanuel Ringelblum is executed with his family.

**August 1944**

Liquidation of Lodz ghetto begins; Chaim and Regina Rumkowski are gassed at Auschwitz-Birkenau.

**September 18, 1946**

First part of Oneg Shabbat Archives is discovered in Warsaw.

# ━⟶ CHAPTER NOTES ⟶━

## Introduction

1. *Funk and Wagnall's Standard Desk Dictionary* in Micro Library CD-ROM (San Jose, Calif.: Inductel, 1991).

2. Martin Luther in George Seldes, *The Great Thoughts* (New York: Ballantine Books, 1985), p. 255.

3. *Fifty Years Ago: Revolt Amid the Darkness* (Washington, D.C.: United States Holocaust Memorial Museum, 1993), p. 17.

## Chapter 1

1. Order No. 15, July 10, 1941, in Avraham Tory, *Surviving the Holocaust: The Kovno Ghetto Diary* (Cambridge, Mass.: Harvard University Press, 1990), p. 17.

2. Chaim A. Kaplan, *Scroll of Agony: The Warsaw Diary of Chaim A. Kaplan* (New York: Macmillan, 1965), p. 59.

3. Ibid., pp. 129–130.

## Chapter 2

1. Archives of the Jewish Historical Institute, Document 31, in Isaiah Trunk, *Judenrat: The Jewish Councils in Eastern Europe Under Nazi Occupation* (Lincoln, Neb.: University of Nebraska Press, 1996), p. 389.

2. Ibid., p. 389.

3. Calel Perechodnik, *Am I a Murderer? Testament of a Jewish Ghetto Policeman* (Boulder, Colo.: Westview Press, 1996), p. 12.

4. Chaim A. Kaplan, *Scroll of Agony: The Warsaw Diary of Chaim A. Kaplan* (New York: Macmillan, 1965), p. 215.

5. Chaim Rumkowski, quoted in Emmanuel Ringelblum, *Notes From the Warsaw Ghetto: The Journal of Emmanuel Ringelblum* (New York: McGraw-Hill Book Co., 1958) p. 126.

6. Zonabend Collection, quoted in Trunk, p. 90.

7. Jacob Gens, in Trunk, p. 403.

8. Ephraim Barasz, in Trunk, p. 402.

9. Perechodnik, p. 9.

10. Kaplan, p. 234.

11. Ringelblum, pp. 154–55.

## Chapter 3

1. Calel Perechodnik, *Am I a Murderer? Testament of a Jewish Ghetto Policeman* (Boulder, Colo.: Westview Press, 1996), p. 22.

2. Lucjan Dobroszycki, ed., *The Chronicle of the Lodz Ghetto 1941–1944* (New Haven, Conn.: Yale University Press, 1984), p. 233.

3. Quoted in Emmanuel Ringelblum, *Notes From the Warsaw Ghetto: The Journal of Emmanuel Ringelblum* (New York: McGraw-Hill Book Co., 1958), p. 208.

4. Dobroszycki, p. 232.

5. Robert N. Proctor, *Racial Hygiene: Medicine Under the Nazis* (Cambridge, Mass.: Harvard University Press, 1988).

6. Report of Ludwig Fischer, quoted in Israel Gutman, *Resistance: The Warsaw Ghetto Uprising* (Boston: Houghton Mifflin, 1994), p. 89.

7. Avraham Tory, *Surviving the Holocaust: The Kovno Ghetto Diary* (Cambridge, Mass.: Harvard University Press, 1990), p. 21.

8. Ringelblum, p. 124.

9. Kaplan, p. 242.

10. Dobroszycki, p. 92.

11. Trunk, p. 226.

12. Dobroszycki, p. 102.

13. Tory, p. 255.

## Chapter 4

1. Martin Gilbert, *The Holocaust: A History of the Jews of Europe During the Second World War* (New York: Holt, Rinehart and Winston, 1985), p. 154.

2. Ibid., p. 175.

3. Otto Ohlendorf, in Lucy S. Dawidowicz, *The War Against the Jews: 1933–1945* (New York: Holt, Rinehart and Winston, 1975), p. 127.

4. Margot Stern Strom and William S. Parsons, *Facing History and Ourselves: Holocaust and Human Behavior* (Watertown, Mass.: Intentional Educations, 1982), p. 208.

5. Israel Gutman, *Resistance: The Warsaw Ghetto Uprising* (Boston: Houghton Mifflin, 1994), p. 102.

6. Abba Kovner, in Gutman, p. 103.

7. Daniel Jonah Goldhagen, *Hitler's Willing Executioners: Ordinary Germans and the Holocaust* (New York: Alfred A. Knopf, 1996), p. 154.

8. Avraham Tory, *Surviving the Holocaust: The Kovno Ghetto Diary* (Cambridge, Mass.: Harvard University Press, 1990), p. 49

9. Adolf Hitler, in George Seldes, *The Great Thoughts* (New York: Ballantine Books, 1985), p. 185.

10. Lucjan Dobroszycki, ed., *The Chronicle of the Lodz Ghetto 1941–1944* (New Haven, Conn.: Yale University Press, 1984), pp. 529–530.

11. Adam Czerniakow, *The Warsaw Diary of Adam Czerniakow: Prelude to Doom* (New York: Stein and Day, 1979) p. 385.

12. Ibid., p. 136.

13. Calel Perechodnik, *Am I a Murderer? Testament of a Jewish Ghetto Policeman* (Boulder, Colo.: Westview Press, 1996), p. 173.

14. Dobroszycki, p. 113.

15. Ibid., p. 113.

16. Chaim Rumkowski, in Isaiah Trunk, *Judenrat: The Jewish Councils in Eastern Europe Under Nazi Occupation* (Lincoln, Neb.: University of Nebraska Press, 1996), p. 423.

17. Jacob Gens, in Isaiah Trunk, *Judenrat: The Jewish Councils in Eastern Europe Under Nazi Occupation* (Lincoln, Neb.: University of Nebraska Press, 1996), p. 421.

## Chapter 5

1. Adam Czerniakow, *The Warsaw Diary of Adam Czerniakow: Prelude to Doom* (New York: Stein and Day, 1979), p. 12.

2. Israel Gutman, *Resistance: The Warsaw Ghetto Uprising* (New York: Houghton Mifflin, 1994), p. 96.

3. Chaim A. Kaplan, *Scroll of Agony: The Warsaw Diary of Chaim A. Kaplan* (New York: Macmillan, 1965), p. 268.

4. Ibid., p. 339.

5. Emmanuel Ringelblum, *Notes From the Warsaw Ghetto: The Journal of Emmanuel Ringelblum* (New York: McGraw-Hill Book Co., 1958), p. 341.

6. Alicia Appleman-Jurman, *Alicia: My Story* (New York: Bantam Books, 1990), p. 34.

7. Ringelblum, p. 342.

8. Martin Gilbert, *The Holocaust: A History of the Jews of Europe During the Second World War* (New York: Holt, Rinehart and Winston, 1985), pp. 549–550.

9. Appleman-Jurman, p. 116.

10. Ibid., p. 139.

11. Ibid., p. 159.

## Chapter 6

1. Quoted in Martin Gilbert, *The Holocaust: A History of the Jews of Europe During the Second World War* (New York: Holt, Rinehart and Winston, 1985), p. 667.

2. Alexander Donat, *The Holocaust Kingdom*, in Albert Friedlander, ed., *Out of the Whirlwind* (New York: Schocken Books, 1976), pp. 175, 176.

3. Isaiah Trunk, *Judenrat: The Jewish Councils in Eastern Europe Under Nazi Occupation* (Lincoln, Neb.: University of Nebraska Press, 1996), p. 450.

4. Emmanuel Ringelblum, *Notes From the Warsaw Ghetto: The Journal of Emmanuel Ringelblum* (New York: McGraw-Hill Book Co., 1958), p. 326.

5. Itzak Zuckerman, quoted in Israel Gutman, *Resistance: The Warsaw Ghetto Uprising* (New York: Houghton Mifflin, 1994), p. 159.

6. Vladka Meed, *On Both Sides of the Wall: Memoirs from the Warsaw Ghetto* (American edition) (Washington, D.C.: Holocaust Library, 1993), p. 76.

7. Ibid., p. 78.

8. Ibid.

9. Gilbert, p. 522.

10. Meed, p. 121.

11. Israel Gutman, *Resistance: The Warsaw Ghetto Uprising* (New York: Houghton Mifflin, 1994), p. xix.

12. Meed, p. 126.

13. Gilbert, p. 557.

14. Zivia Lubetkin, quoted in *Fifty Years Ago: Revolt Amid the Darkness* (Washington, D.C.: United States Holocaust Memorial Museum, 1993), p. 203.

15. Ibid., p. 558.

16. Meed, p. 146.

17. Lubetkin, in *Fifty Years Ago*, p. 207.

18. Gilbert, p. 566.

19. Mordecai Anielewicz, in *Fifty Years Ago*, p. 212.

## Chapter 7

1. Avraham Tory, *Surviving the Holocaust: The Kovno Ghetto Diary* (Cambridge, Mass.: Harvard University Press, 1990), p. 355.

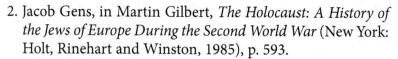

2. Jacob Gens, in Martin Gilbert, *The Holocaust: A History of the Jews of Europe During the Second World War* (New York: Holt, Rinehart and Winston, 1985), p. 593.

3. Abba Kovner, in Gilbert, p. 593.

4. Isaiah Trunk, *Judenrat: The Jewish Councils in Eastern Europe Under Nazi Occupation* (Lincoln, Neb.: University of Nebraska Press, 1996), p. 403.

5. Ibid., p. 468.

6. Bertha Sokolskaya, in Gilbert, p. 599.

# GLOSSARY

**anti-Semitism**—Hostility toward or discrimination against Jews as a religious, ethnic, or racial group.

**Aryans**—Indo-Iranian ancestors of Germans on whom Nazis based their master race claims.

**concentration camp**—An area where the Nazis "concentrated" prisoners in one place, treated them brutally, and forced them to work under subhuman conditions.

**Einsatzgruppen**—Mobile killing units of security police and SD officials.

**fascism**—A form of government headed, in most cases, by a dictator.

**führer**—German national leader; Adolf Hitler was Der Führer of Germany.

**genocide**—The systematic killing of an entire racial, ethnic, political, or religious group.

**gentile**—A person of a non-Jewish nation.

**Gestapo**—The Nazi secret police active in rounding up Jews for the death camps.

**ghettos**—A small, run-down area of a town where Jews, under Nazi persecution, were isolated and forced to live, until they were deported to concentration camps.

**guerrilla warfare**—Fighting tactics which include being aggressive, radical, or unconventional.

**Holocaust**—The systematic extermination of six million European Jews by the Nazis.

**Jewish Fighting Organization** (ZOB)—Established in the ghettos, by the Jews, for the purpose of organizing and obtaining weapons for defense against Nazis.

**Judenrat**—Jewish Council set up in the ghettos, by the Nazis, to ensure all orders for the Jewish movement were carried out.

**judenrein**—Empty (free) of Jews.

**kibbutz**—Communal farm or settlement in Israel.

**kiddush hashem**—Ceremonial blessing pronounced over wine or bread in a Jewish home or synagogue on a holy day.

**Knesset**—Israel parliament.

**Nuremberg Laws**—Laws established on September 15, 1935, wiping out the rights of Germany's Jews.

**Operation Barbarossa**—The German invasion of Russia in World War II.

**SD** (*Sicherheitsdienst*)—The intelligence service of the SS headed by Reinhard Heydrich.

**SS** (*Schutzstaffel*)—"Black Shirts"; Hitler's personal guard unit; expanded in World War II to perform mass killings.

# ⊱FURTHER READING⊰

Appleman-Jurman, Alicia. *Alicia: My Story*. New York: Bantam Books, 1990.

Dobroszycki, Lucjan, ed. *The Chronicle of the Lodz Ghetto: 1941–1944*. New Haven, Conn.: Yale University Press, 1984.

Grossman, Chaika. *The Underground Army*. Washington, D.C.: United States Holocaust Memorial Museum, 1988.

Gutman, Israel. *Resistance: The Warsaw Ghetto Uprising*. Boston: Houghton Mifflin, 1994.

Kaplan, Chaim A. *Scroll of Agony: The Warsaw Diary of Chaim A. Kaplan*. New York: Macmillan, 1965.

Meed, Vladka. *On Both Sides of the Wall: Memoirs from the Warsaw Ghetto*. Washington, D.C.: Holocaust Library, 1993.

Perechodnik, Calel. *Am I a Murderer: Testament of a Jewish Ghetto Policeman*. Boulder, Colo.: Westview Press, 1996.

Ringelblum, Emmanuel. *Notes From the Warsaw Ghetto: The Journal of Emmanuel Ringelblum*. New York: McGraw-Hill Book, Co. 1958.

Tory, Avraham. *Surviving the Holocaust: The Kovno Ghetto Diary*. Cambridge, Mass.: Harvard University Press, 1990.

# INDEX